INTO THE CL

GW00738233

RELIGIOUS EDUCATION IN THE LEAVING CERTIFICATE

Religion
and Science

Fachtna McCarthy
& Joseph McCann

Series Editors
Eoin G. Cassidy and Patrick M. Devitt

VERITAS

First published 2003 by
Veritas Publications
7/8 Lower Abbey Street
Dublin 1
Ireland
Email publications@veritas.ie
Website www.veritas.ie

ISBN 1 85390 694 8

10 9 8 7 6 5 4 3 2 1

Cover design by Bill Bolger
Printed in the Republic of Ireland by Betaprint Ltd, Dublin

*Veritas books are printed on paper made from the wood pulp of managed
forests. For every tree felled, at least one tree is planted, thereby renewing
natural resources.*

Contents

Introduction

September 2003 saw the introduction of the Leaving Certificate Religious Education Syllabus by the Department of Education and Science. For those concerned to promote a religious sensibility in young Irish adults it is hard to exaggerate the importance of this event. It both represents a formal recognition by society of the value of religious education in the academic lives of second-level students, and it also reflects the importance which Irish society attaches to promoting the personal growth of students, including their spiritual and moral development. Religious education offers young people the opportunity to understand and interpret their experience in the light of a religious world-view. Furthermore, in and through an engagement with the RE Syllabus at Leaving Certificate level, students will learn a language that will enable them both to articulate their own faith experience and to dialogue with those of different faiths or non-theistic stances.

The Department of Education Syllabus is to be welcomed in that it gives recognition to the role that religious education plays in the human development of the young person. It is not an exaggeration to say that religious education is the capstone of the school's educational response to the young person's search for meaning and values. In this context, it encourages students to reflect upon their awareness of themselves as unique individuals with roots in a community network of family, friends and parish. Furthermore, it allows students to acknowledge and reflect upon their relationship to a God who cares for them and for the world in which we live. Finally, it gives students access to the universal nature of the quest for truth, beauty and goodness. Most of these themes are addressed sympathetically in the section entitled *The Search for Meaning and Values*. In particular, this section is to be welcomed because it offers the possibility for students to grapple with theistic and non-theistic world-views in a context that is hospitable to religious belief.

A critical dimension of the young person's educational journey is the growth in understanding of their own culture and the manner in which culture shapes their outlook on the world. The Religious Education Syllabus not only addresses the manner in which religion (and in particular Christianity) has shaped Irish culture over many centuries, but it also provides an extremely valuable platform from which to critique aspects of the relationship between faith and culture in the contemporary world. The section entitled *Religion: The Irish Experience* addresses the former concern by showing pupils the manner in which the Christian religion has contributed to the belief patterns and values of Irish society. It also alerts them to the depths of religious belief that predate by many centuries, even millennia, the arrival of Christianity in Ireland; and it also connects them to the cultural richness that links Ireland to the European continent. In this context, the devotional revolution that took place in Ireland (including the extraordinary growth in religious orders from 1850-1930) is a topic that could be expanded. The missionary outreach of the Catholic Church in Ireland in the last hundred years is worthy of special mention. Finally, students studying this section should be encouraged to acknowledge the ambiguities that have attended the presence of religion in Ireland over the centuries; to see on the one hand the image of an island of saints and scholars, and on the other hand to note how 'lilies that fester smell far worse than weeds'.

In examining the manner in which faith and culture interact, the sections entitled *Religion and Science* and *Religion and Gender* make a valuable contribution to the Syllabus. These sections address topical issues that were controversial in the past and continue to be problematical even today. In treating of these two topics it is obviously important to avoid stereotypes – the acceptance of unexamined assumptions that mask or over-simply the truth to such an extent as to do a disservice to the seriousness of the issues involved. Likewise, the section on *World Religions* should be taught in a manner that is sensitive to the dangers of cultural and religious stereotypes. This section not only gives students a valuable introduction to the main religions in the world, but it also provides a cultural context for an awareness of the fact that the phenomenon of religion and the experience of religious belief is something that shapes people's understanding of themselves and their lifestyles across all cultural boundaries. Furthermore, it should never be forgotten that if, as Christians believe, God's Spirit is present in and through these religions, there is a need to study these religions precisely in order to discover aspects of God's presence in the world that has the capability to continually surprise.

In the Irish cultural context, Catholicism shapes the religious sensibilities and practices of the majority of young people. The Syllabus offers a generous acknowledgement of the importance of Christianity in the Irish context by providing two sections that focus on core aspects of the Christian faith. These are: *Christianity: origins and contemporary expressions* and *The Bible: Literature and Sacred text*. In this context, the Syllabus section on the Bible is to be welcomed. However, greater attention could be given to the role and significance of the Prophets in the Old Testament and to Paul in the New Testament. Furthermore, in studying the Bible it should never be forgotten that the primary reality is not the 'book' but rather the person of Christ and the community tradition grappling with this reality that is revealed in and through the Bible.

What is often in danger of being forgotten in an academic context is the importance of the fostering of attitudes and practices that promote personal growth. Religious education cannot be focused only on knowledge and understanding, because religion is primarily a way of celebrating life and, in particular, the spiritual dimension of life in and through the practices of worship, ritual and prayer. The Syllabus's recognition of this critical dimension of religious education through the section entitled *Worship, Ritual and Prayer* is to be welcomed. In addressing this section of the Syllabus it would be important to alert students to the great variety of spiritualities, prayer forms, mysticisms, rituals and styles of music that are to be found within the Christian tradition in order that students may have the possibility of exploring the richness of the spiritual dimension of their own tradition.

A key remit of the educational process is the fostering of moral maturity through a syllabus that allows students to engage in moral education. Not only is religious education particularly suited to facilitating this educational imperative, but the ethical character of human life is a core feature of all religions. The importance of this dimension of religious education is recognised in the provision of two sections entitled *Moral Decision Making* and *Issues of Justice and Peace*. There is nothing optional about the challenge to promote justice and peace. However, it is a topic that can all too easily be ideologically driven. Therefore, there is a special responsibility on those teaching this section to ensure that the instances of injustice cited, and the causes of injustice proposed, are grounded in solid research.

The challenges to Catholic religion teachers

Though religious education has been an integral part of Irish second-level schools long before the foundation of the state, it has not until now been possible to assess this work under the State examination system. The reason for this anomaly is the Intermediate Education Act (1878) which allowed for the teaching but forbade the State examination of religious education. The removal of this legal constraint on State examination of RE has provided the impetus for the introduction of the Junior Certificate Syllabus in September 2000 and the introduction of the Leaving Certificate Syllabus in September 2003. These changes are to be welcomed but they provide a number of major challenges to Catholic religion teachers that should not be minimised.

In the *first* place, Catholic religion teachers have to attend to the danger that the new Syllabus will lead to a weakening of a commitment to catechesis in second level schools. The catechetical project of faith formation is built around six key pillars: knowledge of the faith; liturgical/sacramental education; moral formation; learning to pray; education for community life, including a fostering of the ecumenical character of Christian community, and finally, missionary initiative and inter-religious dialogue. Clearly, the RE Leaving Certificate Syllabus does give attention to many of the above themes, including the key catechetical concerns of attitude or value formation and the development of commitments. However, the emphasis in the Syllabus is undoubtedly upon the acquiring of knowledge, understanding and knowledge-based skills, all of which undoubtedly place it under the rubric of religious education rather than catechesis. The religion teacher ought to value the distinctive approaches to religion reflected in both catechesis and religious education. Both are important because both contribute in distinctive ways to the religious development of the young person. Catechesis aims at maturity of faith whereas religious education aims at knowledge and understanding of the faith.

From the point of view of the religion teacher, the teaching can have a different tone at different times. On one occasion, it might have a 'showing how' or catechetical tone, one that assumes a shared faith experience and encourages active participation. At another time it can have an educational or 'explaining' tone that invites pupils to stand back from religion to a certain extent, so that they can gain a more objective understanding of what is being taught. The Religious Education Syllabus should be taught in a manner that keeps both of these approaches in balance. In a similar vein, the presence of RE on the Leaving Certificate curriculum should not distract teachers from acknowledging that the religious development of young people happens in many contexts, which are distinct, though complementary. It can take place at home, in the parish, with friends as well as in school. Furthermore, even in the school it can take place at a whole series of levels including liturgy, prayer and projects that encourage an awareness of the need to care for those in most need.

In the *second* place, teachers have to attend to the scope and range of the aims of the Syllabus, one that seeks both to introduce students to a broad range of religious traditions and to the non-religious interpretation of life as well as providing students with the opportunity to develop an informed and critical understanding of the Christian tradition. In this context, teachers have to balance the need to promote tolerance for and mutual understanding of those of other or no religious traditions, alongside the need to give explicit attention to the Christian faith claims that Jesus is the Son of God and that he died to save us and to unite us with God and one another. Similarly, in teaching Christianity, teachers need to give attention to the role and significance of the Church from a Catholic perspective. It should never be forgotten that the idea of the Church as 'people of God', 'body of Christ' and 'temple of the Holy Spirit' is one that is at the heart of Catholic self-understanding.

In a similar vein, the Syllabus encourages students to engage critically with a wide variety of ethical codes with a view to the development of a moral maturity. Teachers will have to balance this approach with the way in which morality is viewed within the Christian tradition under the heading of discipleship – Jesus invites people to follow *him* rather than an ethical code or vision. Furthermore, from a Christian perspective, morality is never simply or even primarily concerned with a listing of moral prohibitions, rather it situates the ethical dimension of human nature within the context of a belief in a forgiving God. Finally, it should not be forgotten that it does not make sense to teach morality in too abstract a manner. Morality is something preeminently practical and at all times needs to be brought down to the level of real people – those who struggle with the demands of conscience in their lives. From a Catholic perspective, one has in the lives of the saints a multitude of examples of the manner in which people have attempted to follow the call to discipleship that is Christian morality.

Finally, nobody concerned with the seriousness of the challenge facing schools to promote moral maturity could be unaware of the importance of the contemporary challenge posed to the promotion of societal and religious values by the rise of a relativist and/or subjectivist ethos. In this context, the teaching of the broad variety of moral codes will have to be done in a manner that draws students' attention to the importance of acknowledging the objective nature of morality as opposed to accepting uncritically either a relativist or a subjectivist standpoint. In the light of the need to critique an exaggerated acceptance of pluralism, there is also a need to acknowledge that not all theories are equally valid, and moral decision-making is not simply a matter of applying one's own personal preference.

What is proposed in these commentaries
Given the breadth and scope of the Syllabus it is undoubtedly true that teachers will have to attend to the wide variety of sections in the Syllabus which demand a breadth of knowledge that some may find a little daunting. Even though it is not envisaged that teachers would attempt to teach all ten sections

of the Syllabus to any one group of students, nevertheless, the Syllabus will make demands upon teachers that can only be met if there are support services in place. For example, apart from the need to ensure the publishing of good quality teaching and learning resources, the schools themselves will need to ensure that appropriate resources – books, CDs, internet and videos – are provided. Finally, teachers will need to be provided with appropriate in-service training. It is to furthering this goal of providing good quality teaching and learning resources that the present series of volumes is addressed.

The eleven volumes in this series of commentaries comprise an introductory volume (already published, *Willingly To School*) that reflects upon the challenge of RE as an examination subject, along with ten other volumes that mirror the ten sections in the Syllabus. These commentaries on the Syllabus have been published to address the critical issue of the need to provide resources for the teaching of the Syllabus that are both academically rigorous and yet accessible to the educated general reader. Although primarily addressed to both specialist and general teachers of religion and third-level students studying to be religion teachers, the commentaries will be accessible to parents of Leaving Certificate pupils and, in addition, it is to be hoped that they will provide an important focus for adults in parish-based or other religious education or theology programmes. In the light of this focus, each of the volumes is structured in order to closely reflect the content of the Syllabus and its order of presentation. Furthermore, they are written in clear, easily accessible language and each includes an explanation of new theological and philosophical perspectives.

The volumes offered in this series are as follows

Patrick M. Devitt: *Willingly to School: Religious Education as an Examination Subject*

Eoin G. Cassidy: *The Search for Meaning and Values*

Thomas Norris and Brendan Leahy: *Christianity: Origins and Contemporary Expressions*

Philip Barnes: *World Religions*

Patrick Hannon: *Moral Decision Making*

Sandra Cullen: *Religion and Gender*

John Murray: *Issues of Justice and Peace*

Christopher O'Donnell: *Worship, Prayer and Ritual*

Benedict Hegarty: *The Bible: Literature and Sacred Text*

John Walsh: *Religion: The Irish Experience*

Fachtna McCarthy and Joseph McCann: *Religion and Science*

Thanks are due to the generosity of our contributors who so readily agreed to write a commentary on each of the sections in the new Leaving Certificate Syllabus. Each of them brings to their commentary both academic expertise and a wealth of experience in the teaching of their particular area. In the light of this, one should not underestimate the contribution that they will make to the work of preparing teachers for this challenging project. Thanks are also due to our publishers, Veritas. Their unfailing encouragement and practical support has been of inestimable value to us and has ensured that these volumes saw the light of day. Finally, we hope that you the reader will find each of these commentaries helpful as you negotiate the paths of a new and challenging syllabus.

Eoin G. Cassidy
Patrick M. Devitt
Series Editors

I

The Scientific and Theological Enterprises

1.1 QUESTIONING IN CONTEXT

An overview

One of our deepest human needs is to make sense of our experience, to give a coherent and full account of the world in which we live so that we can be fulfilled and happy in it. It is a quest that science and religion have in common for they are both, in their different ways, trying to explore aspects of the real, the way things are. But they are hardly equal partners in the quest today. There is a sense that science and theology are two completely different spheres of human interest having an uneasy tension between them. Science holds a privileged position in modern culture whereas organised religion is in decline. The media and popular culture reinforce the 'cultural ascendancy' of the sciences as central and predominant. Science and technology have transformed our map of the physical universe and their many powerful applications penetrate every facet of life from the economy to our health and our lifestyles. The world since the rise of science has increasingly pushed religious thinkers to the margin. Theologians and religious philosophers seem to be dealing with the mystical, the spiritual, the personal, the private, the subjective, and the emotional – areas that appear vague and woolly. Empirically based science is the 'hard core of modernity' and provides the dynamic engine of change, constantly revising its conclusions and pushing back the frontiers of knowledge.

Popular stereotypes also get in the way of a proper dialogue between religion and the sciences. There is the image of the 'nerdy', or even the 'mad' scientist, detached from reality, the person in the white coat who speaks in the impenetrable language of higher mathematics. Science is also demonised as the cause of many of our modern ills: the pollution of the planet, the nuclear threat and weapons of mass destruction. While not denying the obvious benefits of scientific research, some blame science for wresting all mystery from the universe, making it a godless place and in the process destroying all human meaning and value. Such negative stereotyping of science and scientists worries educators today because it deters young students from pursuing science subjects in our universities. On the other hand, religious people are sometimes portrayed as well-intentioned do-gooders, a little 'dotty' like 'Father Ted', or 'sky pilots' who are out of touch with the real world.

This polarisation is unfortunate because a division between the religious and scientific spheres can lead to two opposite and quite harmful consequences: an unfeeling and spiritually arid technical view of the world, or an unthinking woolly and ultimately unconvincing spirituality. We need the insights and energy from both areas to achieve a balanced understanding of reality and a humane approach to our life with others in the world. The great physicist Albert Einstein said 'religion without science is blind; science without religion is lame'. Religion without science runs the risk of becoming superstitious and irrational. Science without religion is like an attempt to walk on one foot, a partial vision that sees science as furnishing the only knowledge of reality. Science can make people better but can it make better people? People have to explore the capabilities of the planet for the full development of human life, and at the same time, pay heed to the needs of the human heart and spirit.

We need science and technology and an enthusiasm for discovery and experiment to understand and develop the world. We need philosophy and theology, ethical convictions, religious belief, an ecological ethic, contemplative awareness, and devotion to the human community to nurture the human spirit. Humanity requires both if we are to be successful in resolving the pressing issues before us, many of which will be explored in the following chapters. Our civilisation is facing into very big decisions: about the use of natural resources, about care of the environment, about medical advances, about population control, about the care of sick and elderly people, and about new technologies and procedures in genetics. The opportunities and hazards that await us demand careful reflection and responsible decision-making.

The purpose of this book

What is the place of religion in an age of science? The purpose of this book, then, is to help bring the insights and concerns of these two distinct disciplines together in a mutually constructive dialogue.

There are four parts to the book, responding to one of the following aims:
- to discuss and analyse the nature and methods of the scientific and theological enterprises: Part One
- to tell the story of some key moments in the history of the relationship between religion and science and their importance: Part Two
- to examine some of the emerging and contemporary debates between religion and science and their contexts: Part Three and Part Four

Hence, the first part of the book is about the relationship of science and religion in theory, the second part is about the relationship of science and religion in the past, and the third part is about issues in the relationship of science and religion in the present.

The relationship between science and religion is one of the most fundamental challenges that face the mind and spirit of people today. The contemporary dialogue shows positive and hopeful signs, specifically in the last quarter century in the open climate that lends itself to a constructive debate among scientists and theologians. Scientists and theologians regularly come together to discuss fields of mutual interest, areas of overlap and pressing issues in cosmology, evolution and genetics. Scientists are showing more sensitivity to religious questions and theologians are actively engaging with the implications of modern science for their religious picture of the world. Both scientists and religious people together can face the challenges of our age bringing their respective sources of truth and insight to bear on the human search for a fruitful and fulfilled life.

The human need to question

Wonder is the beginning of knowledge. Wonder is the human urge to find out things, to explore, to satisfy our natural curiosity. Our minds come programmed to question and to wonder, to look behind the obvious, to explore further, to find out what makes something work. Developmental psychologists have come to believe recently in the 'child as scientist'. Even by the age of two, in fact, at the same time as they learn to talk, children are asking the entire range of questions. If we want to put it more technically, there is within the human heart an irrepressible and unrestricted desire to know and to love. This desire is awakened by questions like what? how? where? when? and why? These questions are provoked by the great variety of experiences that humans undergo, experiences of good and evil, joy and sorrow, love and betrayal and suffering and death. It is natural for human beings to wonder about life and destiny, where they have come from and where they are going. The Greek philosopher Plato had a wonderful image of the restless human quest for meaning and fulfilment. We are like 'leaky vessels' into which we keep pouring experiences. Nothing in the world of things ever fulfils us as everything leaks away, nothing lasts, nothing ultimately satisfies. Relationships fulfil us and make us happy, but they can be fragile and fleeting. In the midst of imperfect loves and wounded relationships we experience a drive beyond the limited toward transcendence, for that which ultimately satisfies. St Augustine summed up this drive toward transcendence in the words, 'you have made us for yourself O Lord and our hearts are restless until they rest in you'. Both science and religion offer answers and explanations, or at least descriptions and accounts, which attempt to answer the whole range of questions.

Broadly speaking, science seeks to answer the 'how' question and religion addresses 'why' questions. Science analyses and interprets the data of the natural world and religion interprets the data of human experience and history from within a community of faith. Religion is concerned with ultimate questions of meaning and purpose: why do I exist rather than not exist? Does life make sense? Is there a God, and if so, what kind of God? What is the ground of order, beauty and intelligibility in the world? Why be moral? Do evil and injustice have the final word in life? Why bother to search for truth? All the world religions have in common the search for a meaningful and fulfilled life and bring a religious vision and moral traditions to bear on that search.

The natural sciences are concerned with understanding the structure and composition of the physical world around us. Science accepts the givenness of the real world and asks, what is there? What is the relationship between what is there, and what laws or principles describe these relations? A working definition of science run as follows: the discovery of knowledge about the natural world that is empirical, inductive, systematic, and rational. Science in its methodology steers clear of matters of moral value, quality, meaning and purpose.

Questions common to science and religion
Perhaps the distinction is too neat, as there are borderline questions and areas of overlap between science and religion.

Questions common to science and religion include questions about origins/beginnings and conclusions/endings. The science of cosmology studies the origin and evolving structure of the material universe, how it all began and what will become of it in the future. The religious doctrine of creation speaks of the universe as God's creation and its continuing dependency on him for its existence. Eschatology is the religious teaching on the future of the world and God's plan for the final destiny of human beings. Questions on human evolution in biology often appear to be at odds with the biblical vision of humans created in the image and likeness of God. Historically, as we shall see, answers offered by the one posed questions for the other, often as a result of misunderstandings and confusion as to their proper roles. Formulating the correct questions is therefore indispensable to both enterprises. Many of the historical disputes between both could be attributed to the blurring of religious with scientific questions and vice versa. Holmes Rolston said, 'questions tell us what to look for, what to discount, what to make of what we find; and in this sense, they are proposals as well as discoveries'.

Science and religion continually struggle against the temptation to fundamentalism, against a hardening of attitudes, a tendency to overplay their hand and to claim more for their discipline than is warranted. In science this temptation is manifested in 'scientism', which claims that science is competent to explain everything and can provide us with the only reliable knowledge. Religious fundamentalists base their world-view on the absolute truth found in a religious revelation, rejecting the findings of science and reason where they clash with a literal interpretation of their religious texts.

'God of the Gaps'

A classic historical example of confusion between science and religion is the so-called 'God of the Gaps'. The phrase describes the mistaken policy of locating God's action in those phenomena of the natural world for which science was not yet able to give a satisfactory account. God is located in the gaps not yet explained by science. For example, in ancient times thunder was interpreted as an expression of God's anger whereas now it can be explained by meteorology. A religion relying on such gaps is then forced into retreat when the gaps are eventually filled by scientific explanation. Isaac Newton's universe required God, by means of the 'divine arm', to perform minor adjustments to the orbits of the planets. Such an impoverished God, restricted to filling in the scientifically unexplained parts of the universe, was gradually squeezed out altogether, as the gaps got smaller and smaller. As we shall see, it led, unintentionally, to the rise of atheism. Theology today looks for evidence of God's action *within* natural processes, rather than apart from them.

Two other images of God and their implications for science
The way we understand God and his action in the world, as illustrated by the God of the gaps, has implications for our scientific picture of the universe. An erroneous or inadequate image of God has often been at the hidden core of disputes between religion and science in the past. For Thomas Aquinas, the great medieval Christian theologian, God is profoundly mystery. God in his essence is incomprehensible and unknowable to us because he is the Creator of all that is, and there is a deep ontological gap between creatures and their Creator. He is outside the order of beings and objects in the world, and so he cannot be classified as any kind of being. He is the reason why there exists a universe at all. God is in everything holding it constantly in existence, but he is not located anywhere. Aquinas was fond of saying that we do not know *what* God is, only *that* he is (exists) and what he is not. The incomprehensibility of God may give the impression that there is very little we can say about him at all, as we do not know what the word 'God' means. For Aquinas, we can know

something about God from his effects, from the creatures he has made. Creation is fundamentally a relationship between God and his creatures. Creatures have being as a participation in God's absolute Being.

The great monotheistic traditions (Judaism, Christianity, and Islam) see God as actively sustaining the order of the physical universe, that God continues to sustain the laws, which govern the regularity of the cosmos. The creator intends to make himself known to his creatures and, in fact, one main reason why there is a universe at all is to create beings that can find happiness in knowing and loving God and in co-operating with the creator.

But how does God act in a world so well described by science? The classical Christian view developed by Thomas Aquinas, based on the idea of 'double agency', distinguished between primary and secondary causality. God is the primary cause of all that exists and he works through the secondary causes of the natural world, which science studies. God's sovereignty over nature is exercised always through the use of secondary causes, through natural laws and human agency, to achieve his purposes, without infringing on the freedom of his creatures. This means that God's activity is always mediated through secondary causes. He does not interfere with the laws of nature; rather, God acts to devise and implement the laws that generate new patterns of complex beauty and order. The two kinds of causality are required for a complete description of the real, but they are on a completely different level; scientific and theological explanations are independent of one another. We cannot say *how* God acts because divine causation is very different. There is no 'causal joint' between God's action and events in the natural world and there are no gaps in their scientific account. God acts 'behind' the systems of cause and effect at a level not amenable to physical description.

Karl Rahner, a Christian theologian of the recent past, addressed the question of how we are to speak of God in the context of the dynamic and evolutionary universe understood by science today. His image of God is as the permanent co-presence or omnipresence of God to the world. He argues that whenever we become conscious of ourselves or of other beings in the world, we are also aware in a dim, pre-conceptual way of the limitless mystery that surrounds the world. It is the nature of the material universe to develop toward consciousness as it has a God-given tendency toward self-transcendence. God operates within an evolutionary universe inviting it toward self-transcendence. This means that evolutionary changes happen through natural powers intrinsic to the creature, a process discovered by science; yet, that power ultimately belongs not to the nature of the creature but to the Creator.

The value of this image of God is that it does not interfere with developments or discoveries in science, and at the same time allows religion to speak about the presence of God in the world. Theology sees God, not as being opposed to the world or interfering in its workings, but in treating all that exists within the horizon of God as its origin and its end. 'Horizon' is a helpful metaphor to describe the presence of God; as the horizon that surrounds us and invites us into the future, God is not far from us. We do not 'see' the horizon, but it is the backdrop against which we see everything else. God is not an object within the world, and hence not the concern of science, but he is the beyond, the horizon over against which the limitations of everything in the world are exposed.

1.2   Communities of Inquiry

The importance of community for theology and science

A community is a group of people, who, while sharing common ideas, occupying the same territory, and participating in common practices, come to regard themselves as distinct and distinctive. The scientific and theological traditions of learning, though extended over time and space, each fulfil this description. A member of the community of learning, either in the sciences or in theology, is heavily socialised. Science as a human activity is not done in a vacuum. It is affected by the wider cultural context, by social, moral and spiritual questions of the age. Christopher Southgate writes: 'Science, like theology, needs to be seen as an activity of a community of motivated believers, holding core assumptions and testing out new possibilities'. The community aspect of scholarship both for scientists and theologians needs emphasising. This community is the reference group for the scholar; very often it is consensus among peers that decides whether a scientific theory is accepted where there is a dispute between theories. It is to the community of scholars that the individual researcher looks for affirmation, recognition, and acknowledgement. It is on the scholars of the past or present that the researcher depends for data, hypotheses, and inspiration. The researcher will regard as companions in the quest, not contemporaries and colleagues, but intellectual fellows on the far side of the world. Scientists and academics are cosmopolitans, not locals, members of communities that transcend college corridor and the parish-pump.

Theology is obviously a communal activity in that it studies the shared faith of a community as that is experienced and lived by believers. It tries to give a coherent account of God's revelation as it was received by the original community and passed on in tradition, and how that tradition now engages with contemporary experience. Our experience of the life of faith comes from participation in a community of faith, in is rituals, worship and moral life. If there is no shared experience, we will be unable to communicate. If there is no shared meanings or shared values, we will be at cross-purposes. This means that religion is not a private affair; we do not go to God on our own, but with and through one another in community. It is the faith of the community in a given era that is the object of theology.

Another influential community factor that affects contemporary science is that all scientific activity takes place within a social context. A variety of interests (government, industry, commerce, and education) support and sponsor science with money and resources. Great universities depend on scientists and their research to attract funding. Many pressures weigh on scientists to direct their research in one way or another. There are more important areas of medicine, more productive problems in physics, more useful challenges in chemistry, and non-scientists tell scientists which they are. For example, military needs have often dictated the direction in which research should explore. Scientists well understand which scientific fields will better repay exploration, which can be exploited more easily, and which will lead to the greater rewards. The scientific community approves and authorises what it regards as genuine science.

Objective or subjective investigation

'Objective' investigation claims to approach its subject matter in a neutral, detached and value-free manner, seen as the hallmark of science. Objectivity in science eliminates personal differences among observers and elicits agreement among observers as to the facts. 'Subjective' investigation addresses its subject matter out of a prior commitment and a value-laden position, often associated with a religious faith. In reality, both religion and science have both objective and subjective elements in their approaches, as it is next to impossible to divorce them from each other. There is no bird's eye view of science or religion, as the view from nowhere, outside personal experience, the laboratory or the oratory, history and culture. The popular view of science is the view from nowhere, which enables us to study reality without bias, with a pure objectivity that proves conclusively what is true and what is not. This is a very naïve outlook on science as it reflects an account of scientific method within a narrow rationality that is heavily criticised today. A pure, neutral rationality untouched by commitment and perspective is now widely accepted as an elusive ideal. The notion of the scientist as neutral spectator is no longer viable, particularly in the light of recent scientific discoveries like the 'anthropic principle' and the role of the observer at the quantum level, aspects which will be examined in part three.

Scientific method and theories of interpretation

A key factor in understanding theology and science is that they are both informed by theories of interpretation and that these theories of interpretation are shaped by their respective communities of inquiry, their social and historical contexts. Both science and religion employ the language of models, metaphors and paradigms. To this extent they rely on the art of interpretation and the exercise of the imagination. We will now look at both in turn, beginning with scientific method.

The method of science follows a process of observation and experimentation, hypothesis, testing or verification, interpretation and theory. The inductive method of science is 'bottom-up' thinking. It begins with the most concrete and particular and seeks to find more general patterns to account for the data, which are then expressed in a theory. Science begins with observation and data. The data or observations are precisely measured and recorded. Measurement and the language of measurement, mathematics, provide the most distinguishing mark of modern science. The natural sciences measure the physical properties of the material universe such as temperature, pressure, mass, energy and power. Some experimentation may be required which may involve one or both, observation or measurement. So the first scientific phase is observation and measurement.

Then a supposition or hypothesis is suggested. Maybe it is the case that the individual things that we have seen are the result of some cause or general state of affairs that accounts for the way they are. In other words, the inquirer observes the world as a process, a flow of change, a sequence of events, and then wants to find out how what has been observed happened to come about. This is a creative period because the observer must now imagine what might have happened, what did not happen, and crucially, what may happen in the future. This is the second phase of the scientific investigation: the proposal of hypotheses.

Then the classic scientific moment arrives. At this point, the investigator has a good hunch or guess as to why things are the way they are – a hypothesis. The scientist must find instances where the hypothesis can be disproved or falsified. He or she looks for instances, an observation or an experiment, where the hypothesis does not hold. If none can be found and it survives the test, the hypothesis is not falsified but is considered supported by the evidence. A well-supported hypothesis that has stood repeated testing and requires a status among the scientific community is called a scientific theory.

This pattern of scientific method is the ideal that often does not happen in practice. The scientist is supposed to observe neutrally and without an agenda, and then the next step is to propose a hypothesis to explain what he or she is observing. In practice the procedure is circular. Observations are always with an agenda. 'Seeing is always a theory-laden undertaking', according to Russell Hansen. Observation is a purposeful activity. We have an idea in our head before we begin to look; as a result our hypothesis is already directing our observation. Rather than the hypothesis following from our observation, the hypothesis is to an extent driving the observation.

Modern science is characterised by observation, measurement, prediction and control and from these it acquires its power and value. The questions that science asks are in terms of these four characteristics. Governments rise and fall on percentage point changes in the interest rates. The temperature of our bodies, the pollen count in our atmosphere, the pollution concentration in our waters, the acidity of our soils, the level of poverty in our population, each is a key indicator of a problem in modern life, and all are results of scientific measurement. Science strives to express its questions and answers very precisely, and the most precise way is in numbers and statistics.

Science leads to prediction. The test of what the scientist knows is the capacity to predict, to say what is going to happen next. This is because they hope to have discovered what associations and connections there are between things, in particular what are the necessary and sufficient causes that account for what they observe. So scientific description is not just close observation, it is also explanation that reveals the operators, the factors, or the causes of things. And the proof of finding the cause is being able to predict the future.

The purpose of science is often technological, that is, hands-on control. It is not true to say that science always emerges in technology; sometimes scientists do research simply to find an answer for the intellectual enjoyment of knowing. But more often than not, knowledge is power. Technology is the application of science to practical problems and has overtones of progress or improvements of some kind for people. 'Know-how' becomes 'can-do'. Prediction, of course, is in itself a kind of control. If we know when the rain will come, we have control and choices.

Paradigm shift
The popular view is that science progresses in a gradual unfolding and developmental way, advancing step by step by single discoveries, making steady improvements through history. But the history of science shows that scientists change their theories, not piece-meal, bit by bit, but at 'one fell swoop' in surprising revolutions of thinking. Great change comes not by many small steps, but by sudden large jumps. Radical transformation, rather than steady evolution, is often the way of progress. This is the point of Thomas Kuhn's important

study in 1962, *The Structure of Scientific Revolutions.*

The phrase 'paradigm shift' communicates a feeling for the process. A 'paradigm' is a framework of ideas and concepts comprehensively explaining a field of study. Thomas Kuhn defined paradigms as '... universally recognised scientific achievements that for a time provide model problems and solutions to a community of practitioners.' While a particular paradigm holds, science proceeds 'normally', in general following the rational pattern we have described already. But when the generally recognised pattern begins to fall apart, a new 'paradigm' can suddenly emerge, which overthrows the old ideas in a stunning reversal of all the principles and propositions that made up the old framework. The older paradigm was held in place for a period of years by the loyalty and long-standing practices of the world of scientists. When it is finally discredited, it falls apart all at once.

A well-known example of scientific paradigm shift was the transition from the medieval earth-centred world-view to the sun-centred view of Copernicus. Others were revolutionary ideas in the late nineteenth and early twentieth centuries: Darwin's evolutionary theory, and Einstein's theory of relativity. These massive shifts in scientific thought and general culture are central to the historical story of science's challenge to religion, and are the subject of Part Two of this book.

Theories of interpretation in science

Critical realism

The question of interpretation is central to the philosophy of science. The contemporary debate focuses on what science is and how it relates to the real. The commonly accepted philosophical position is called 'critical realism', and is opposed to 'instrumentalism'. Critical realism means that we accept that there is a real world out there independent of or thought but we can only have a limited and provisional knowledge of it. We cannot simply read off the nature of the world from scientific data. Scientific views depend on prior presuppositions and preconceptions about the world, which in turn affect our selection of what we count as data and the ways in which we interpret the data. We have already noticed the circular nature of scientific method. Realists accept that data are theory-laden and there is also an 'underdetermination' of theory by experiment. We can never prove absolutely a theory to be true, as in pure mathematics; we can only show that in repeated experiments under differing conditions we can say in all the instances examined, it is not false. Critical realism enunciates three 'criteria of reasonableness' to ensure the best fit between our data and the real we are trying to explain. They are: the internal coherence of the theory, that there are no contradictions; its comprehensiveness in accounting for all known data; its economy, meaning the simpler and the more compact the theory, the better. We are 'realistic' about our knowledge, seeking the best fit between scientific data and reality, but we are also 'critical' of it, in the sense that we recognise the provisional nature of our theories, which are subject to revision and change.

Instrumentalism

The challenge to the critical realist position in science comes from 'instrumentalism' or 'constructivism'. This is the claim that science is simply a social construction, a useful way of dealing with the world, rather than an attempt to describe reality. The reason is, not because scientific methods are limited and scientific conclusions are provisional, but because the truth about reality is beyond us. Since we cannot engage with the world at all except through language, concepts and theory there is no way we can get behind our theorising to judge how adequate any theory is to the real. Some philosophers of science today maintain that we can make no realist claims about science at all. Science is very successful and hence very useful for working with the real world, but not for really knowing anything about reality. Scientific data are merely conceptual constructs. The main weakness with this interpretation of science is that it is reflexive, meaning that it rebounds on itself. If all human analysis is socially constructed, so must the social constructivist view of science itself suffer from the same criticism.

Theology and theories of interpretation

Theology comes from the Greek meaning 'word about God' or 'God-talk' or 'God knowledge'. The time-honoured definition of theology is 'faith seeking understanding'. Theology is the discipline that reflects, from within a faith-commitment, on God's revelation embedded in the religious experience and tradition of a community. The method of theology follows a commitment to some form of revelation and faith as found in sacred texts, such as the Hebrew Bible, the New Testament or the Qur'an, and in religious rituals. Theology embodies a living tradition that is correlated with contemporary human experiences and practices. A difficulty for theology is the nature of its subject matter. 'God', as the proper object of theology is incomprehensible and transcendent, is not amenable to observation and experiment. God, as the ultimate mystery that grounds reality, is not an object open to inspection by some scientific technique.

When theology speaks about God and the things of faith it uses the method of analogy. By using models, metaphors and symbols drawn from experience, we move from the known to the unknown to arrive at a more comprehensive expression of what faith means. The Christian claim is that God is Triune and has revealed his true nature in the person of Jesus of Nazareth in history, as told in the Bible and in particular in the Gospels of the New Testament. That revelation is passed on, not only in the Bible, but also in a living tradition down the centuries. We read the Bible today in the light of the tradition handed down to us in the Christian community. Theology interprets the revealed teaching of the sacred scripture to believers; this involves translating the received revelation into contemporary culture. It tries to show the coherence of revelation and defends its religious beliefs against the sometimes hostile cultures in which it is embedded.

The Bible speaks of the personal God of revelation as being also the creator of the universe. Christian faith experiences the universe as one creation, the gift of a gracious God. It celebrates its sense of the divine presence within creation in sacramental forms of worship. As we have seen, God is not a part of the scientific attempt to explain the basic nature of the physical universe, the way the world is. Nevertheless, if God is the creator of the world, it is only to be expected that the discoveries of the sciences will give us a deeper understanding of the creator. 'Natural theology' is the name given to the effort of reason in philosophy to come to know God the creator through reflection on creation. The first scientists in the seventeenth century, like Galileo and Newton, were Christians who pursued their science in order to trace the wisdom and rationality of the creator in the 'book of nature', his works.

Theology is contextual in that it seeks to speak to people of today in the context of the radically new world-view presented by science. We live in a dynamic universe that is in one great process of evolutionary emergence. An expanding universe, an evolutionary world, and a holistic view of reality, means that our theology must make connections. 'Faith seeking understanding' means faith seeking connections with the cosmological and ecological understanding of our world. Theology, then, has to promote a new sense of human belonging, to relate to the new story of our cosmic and biological origins and of our ecological responsibilities, the story told by science.

Ways of relating science and religion

What is the place of religion in an age of science? There are different schemes or typologies by which participants in the dialogue understand the relationship between religion and science today. Three principal ways or models of outlining the relationship are proposed here: conflict, independence, and interaction. Ian Barbour neatly summed up the differing relationships as enemies, strangers or partners. The conflict model centres on the claim that science has overcome religion and replaced it – they are enemies. The independence model claims that religion and science are valid but very different areas of discourse and should be kept apart in their own separate spheres – they are strangers. The interaction model suggests that science and religion inevitably interact, and dialogue is mutually beneficial – they are friends. We shall discuss each in turn in more detail.

Conflict

The underlying assumption in this model is that religion and science are in direct competition with one another; they are answering the same questions and so are on collision course for the best explanation of the real world. Its exponents would claim that science has triumphed over religion. The conflict model is based on the 'warfare' view of history, that science arose in the late medieval period in the teeth of opposition by traditional, authoritarian views of the world based on religious belief. The trial of Galileo and the controversy about Darwin and evolutionary theory are often mentioned as reinforcing the conflict model. History teaches that the more science progresses, the more the power of religion diminishes.

An example of the conflict model is the physicist Peter Atkins. He maintains that modern cosmology excludes the notion of the world being created by God. We don't need a Supreme Being to explain why the universe exists as Big Bang theory in science eliminates the need for God. The view that scientific explanation excludes God's action is summed up by the student who states, 'Genesis says the world was made by God, but we know now it was made by the Big Bang'. Neo-

Darwinists such as Richard Dawkins also subscribe to the conflict model. For him, biological evolution is in direct competition with the 'God hypothesis' to explain the origins of life on earth. Biological science has vanquished all religious explanations. We shall examine Dawkins' thesis in more detail in 2.3.

What both have in common is a certain philosophical interpretation of science calls 'scientism'. Scientism claims that science is the arbiter of all truth. Science provides us with a complete description of reality and supplies the only reliable knowledge about our world. The only meaningful knowledge is what can be empirically tested. What science cannot tell us we cannot know. Religion fails the test and is condemned as subjective and irrational.

Underpinning this model is a philosophy of 'reductionism'. The reductionist view holds that any whole system can be exhaustively explained by an account of its constituent parts. So a human being is 'nothing but' a conglomeration of molecules and atoms, which can be fully understood by the laws of physics and chemistry. The classic reductionist statement comes from Jacques Monod: 'the cell is a machine, the animal is a machine, man is a machine'. This is a purely materialist account of life, that humans are nothing but pieces of biological machinery. The claim that science provides an exhaustive description of reality is an alternative 'faith', scientific materialism. Scientific materialism claims that matter is the only reality and excludes the non-material, such as mind, spirit or God.

For many in the debate today, the 'deification' of science in scientism and reductionism and its claim to explain everything is an untenable interpretation of science. Reductionism is a legitimate part of scientific method (analysing something into its parts) but it is illegitimate to inflate it into a philosophy about the world itself. We can give a very complete biological account of the human being, but to claim we are 'nothing but' what biology tells us is not a scientific claim, but a questionable metaphysical theory. We must distinguish between matters of biology and the philosophical ideas uncritically attached to them. Higher functions cannot be completely understood in terms of lower functions. Thinking is more than electrical waves in the brain. Those elements that get left out in scientific description, for example, love, friendship, emotion, aesthetic sensibility, tend to be defined as less real than the mathematical equations which describe the world in which they arise. Science is not the only way of thinking about our experience and there can be more than one possible explanation. Failure to distinguish between scientific and philosophical questions is at the root of the conflict model. The conflict model promotes the infallibility of science and the inadequacy of religion. Science, in effect, has replaced religion.

The other and opposite outcome of the conflict model sees religion as the victor in the battle between them. Creation scientists or creationists take their stance on the literal truth of the Bible. The Bible offers a better scientific picture of the origins of life and the universe than contemporary cosmology and evolutionary theory. Evolution theory is dismissed as incompatible with the story of creation in the book of Genesis. We shall look at creationism in more detail in section 3.1

Independence
This model argues that the conflict way reveals a fundamental misunderstanding of the real nature of science and religion and a false reading of their history. Only a strict separation of both can do justice to their equally valid, but very different approaches, to the real world. Science and theology belong to separate territories, with strict boundaries between them. Confusion arises when one or other oversteps the frontier and refuses to recognise their respective limitations. They have very dissimilar tasks, they ask different questions, and their methods are very different. Science and religion speak two different languages, which are complementary, but there can be no real conflict as they occupy

two totally different domains of knowledge. Theology is based on God's revelation in history and is concerned with personal questions of a way of life, in the search for meaning, purpose and value in the light of God's revelation. Science is based on human observation, experiment and reason; it tells us how the natural world works and is concerned with prediction and control. There is no conflict between science and religion if we keep them in watertight compartments.

A classic exponent of the independence model is the twentieth-century Protestant theologian Karl Barth. He insists on a rigid separation between science and theology. Science is about the human investigation of the natural world; theology is about responding to God's self-revelation in history. God is totally distinct from the world and methods used to study the world are not applicable to the study of God. Barth denies we can know anything of God from nature, the domain of science. He was a great opponent of natural theology, the idea that we can argue to God from reflecting on the natural world. To do so would contradict the priority of divine revelation and would result in an impoverished and idolatrous God of reason.

Another example of the independence model is the Harvard zoologist Stephen Jay Gould. In a recent book, *Rock of Ages*, he argues that the conflict between science and religion is only a phoney war and exists only when the two camps stray into the territory of the other. His calls his solution NOMA, for Non-Overlapping Magisteria. *Magisterium* is the Latin word for teaching. *Noma* allows science and religion to coexist peacefully in a tolerant and respectful non-interference in one another's affairs. Science defines the natural world; religion defines our moral world, in recognition of their separate spheres on influence. Science is incapable of deciphering the meaning of life, no matter how many advances in brain science or genetics. Religion cannot dismiss the findings of cosmology or biological evolution in the name of Biblical teaching, as the creationists try to do.

The separation model has the advantage of avoiding conflict and appears to be a reasonable way of respecting the contribution of both disciplines, but at the cost of any interaction. Many participants in the dialogue are unhappy with the independence model, not least as it ignores the actual history of the relationship between science and religion. The influence in history goes both ways. Prevailing scientific theories and world-views have always influenced theology. Newton's mechanical universe influenced his vision of God and the way God acts in the world. Likewise, theological presuppositions were frequently woven into scientific theories. It has often been claimed that the Christian doctrine of creation provided the underpinning for the rise of science in the sixteenth century. The belief that the world is ordered and reliable is essential to science; an intelligent and good God creates such a rational and consistent world that is distinct from God and is intelligible to us in science. The interaction between science and religion is always ongoing but may not be explicitly recognised.

Apart from ignoring history, the independence model appears to ignore the human desire to unify our knowledge, to see connections and integrate all our knowledge in a more holistic vision. Separation seems artificial and prevents any constructive interaction, any relationship or dialogue between them. It may be detrimental to theology to immunise it from exposure to the scientific picture; theology contributes to public discourse in that it has things to say about the nature of the real world. To do so, and for the sake of its intellectual integrity in the market place of ideas, it must engage in dialogue or risk being marginalised. It may not be possible to compartmentalise our minds into scientific and religious spheres. As one scientist said, somewhat tongue in cheek, that he was a believer in Church but an atheist in his laboratory. Such a splitting of our knowledge into two mutually exclusive compartments is hardly tenable in our growing consciousness of living in one interconnected world. The separation model does not do justice to the range and depth of issues raised in the actual interface between science and religion today.

Interaction

Many contemporary scientists and theologians are engaged in an attempt to rethink the relationship between religion and science. The climate is more favourable as many of the old hostilities between them have lessened with the passage of time. There is a new interest in dialogue, in search for points of contact, for areas of overlap and parallels in their methods. The distinction between the disciplines is maintained; nevertheless science and religion cannot be artificially insulated from one another as they are both trying to understand the same reality. Fraser Watts asserts that both 'refer in their different ways to aspects of the same real world, and because of this they cannot be regarded as unconnected discourses'. The interaction model proposes a mutually beneficial dialogue: scientific knowledge can broaden the horizon of religious faith and the perspective of religious faith can deepen our understanding of the universe described by science.

There are questions that arise in science that cannot be answered within science itself and on which religion can shed some light. Two of these 'limit' questions on the boundary of science which raise religious issues are: the intelligibility of the universe and the moral responsibility of scientists. The first is the question raised by Albert Einstein: why is the world so intelligible to us? The laws of physics wonderfully explain the workings of the universe. But how do we explain science? Why is the universe orderly and intelligible? The ultimate presuppositions of scientific inquiry are raised in the philosophy of science. Science makes an 'act of faith' in the rationality, the intelligibility, and the contingency of the physical universe. These are unproven and taken for granted by scientists; without them there could be no

science, if the world behaved in chaotic and unpredictable ways
unintelligible to us. For religious people, the intelligibility and
rationality of the universe requires an ultimate rational ground in
God; the rational universe is not accidental but the product of a
Mind. Cosmology and physics also raise the question of
contingency. Why is there a universe at all? Why is there
something rather than nothing at all? The very existence of the
universe, the fact that it need not be, requires an explanation.
Science cannot answer these questions but theology can in the
person of a creator God. Also, moral questions arise for scientists
in the ethical responsibilities they have towards the common
good, specifically from the consequences of research, especially
in the area of genetics, nuclear power and ecology. What is
technically possible may not be morally right.

Some scientists who are also theologians want to push
further than dialogue in the search for 'consonance' between
science and theology. Ian Barbour, Arthur Peacocke, and John
Polkinghorne are some of the scientist-theologians, who have
an expertise in both disciplines, and who are engaged in the
search for consonance. Consonance means the search for a
harmony or a correspondence between what the latest science
says about the world and what theology understands to be
God's creation. Consonance is inspired by recent philosophical
discussions comparing the nature and methods of science and
theology. The ways of science and theology are not nearly so
divergent as the independence or conflict model suggested.
Science is no longer considered to be purely objective and
detached; neither is theology seen as subjective and non-
evidential. The supporters of consonance suggest much closer
parallels in their methods, and in the language of models,
metaphor and analogies, which they both use. Many scientist-
theologians draw strong parallels between scientific and
theological method in their assertion that theology is also a
'critical realist' discipline. Science and theology share certain
characteristics:

- both try to depict the real world
- both do so in metaphorical language and models to interpret their data
- both their understandings of the real are limited and partial
- both provide complementary perspectives on the same reality

Theology also has data constituted by the religious experience of the faith-community; it attempts to give the best explanation of the data and submits these to testing through the criteria of reasonableness. There are disputes as to what constitutes the 'data' of a religion that corresponds to those of science. They may be the scriptures of a religion, or the religious experience or the practices of the community.

At one time science's attempt to provide objectivity and ensure that all evidence was theory-free was presented as the main difference between scientific and religious methods. As we have seen, objectivity in science is problematic. The way data are collected and the criteria by which they are analysed are bound up with existing theories. Religion offers a framework of beliefs with which to interpret experience and makes claims about the nature of the universe, the way things are. Both provide very different but complementary perspectives on the real world.

The notion of complementarity is also reinforced by the role given to models and metaphors in both science and religion. A model is a comparison drawn between something familiar and a more complex reality that we are trying to understand. Models are simplified representations, 'visual aids' to help visualise the area we are studying. A classic example in science was imagining the atom as a miniature solar system, with electrons circling round a nucleus like planets around the sun. A model proves a helpful 'heuristic' device in that it includes mathematical equations that describe its behaviour, and enables calculations and predictions to be made. As well as similarities there are obvious differences between the model and what it depicts. The solar system model proves useful in some situations but not in others, for example in describing the movement of an electron in quantum mechanics. All models are then provisional in character. Modern science uses metaphorical language to describe conceptually difficult phenomena, which are not accessible to our senses such as 'black holes' or 'big bang' or 'selfish gene'. It made quite a difference in history to model the universe as an organism, like the ancient Greeks, or as a machine, like the scientists of the eighteenth century.

The language of models and metaphors is also prominent in theology. We have noted the difficulty of talking about God in a meaningful way. 'God' can only be spoken about by stretching human language, for example, when the Bible says God is a 'shepherd' or a 'rock'. All metaphors contain an 'is and is not'. 'God is a shepherd' expresses the loving care and concern for his people, but he is not literally a man with a crook and his people are not sheep. St Augustine proposed a psychological model to help throw light on the Christian mystery of the Trinity. The relationship between Father, Son and Holy Spirit is like, and yet unlike, the relation between memory, understanding and will in the human mind.

The interaction thesis maintains that theology and science offer compatible, not contradictory, explanations. There are different levels or types of explanations, which do not exclude one another. There is always more than one understanding and one explanation of the world we live in, and the existence of these different layers of understanding accounts for some of the differences between science and religion. Three different types of explanation emerge: interpretative explanation answers the question What?; descriptive explanation answers the question How?; reason-giving explanation answers the question Why? To confuse scientific explanations of origins with religious explanations of divine agency is to commit what Michael Poole calls a 'type-error'. A scientific account of origins in Big Bang theory does not exclude the action of a purposive creator.

A more helpful way of thinking of the relationship between religion and science is in terms of the metaphor of different 'maps' of the one reality. There are different but equally valid, equally real maps of the one world: geological, climatic, economic, demographic and so on. The metaphor of differing maps may be a more fitting way of looking at the scientific and theological description of our one world. It allows for independence from one another, and yet room for dialogue, areas of overlap and even border disputes. Each branch of science will have its own map and its own relations to the various maps the theologians draw. For example, evolution and creation could be seen as two differing, but not necessarily exclusive maps of reality. For John Haught, religion confirms the scientific enterprise, not by answering scientific questions, but by confirming the scientist's belief in the coherence and intelligibility of the real world. The scientist's trust is grounded in a more fundamental frame of reference, in a creator God of love and promise.

Select bibliography

Barbour, I. *When Science Meets Religion*, London: SPCK, 2000

Haught, J. *Science and Religion,* New York: Paulist Press, 1995

McCarthy, F. 'The Mind of God: Science and Theology Today', in Eoin G. Cassidy (ed.), *Faith and Culture in the Irish Context*, Dublin: Veritas, 1996, 35-54

Polkinghorne, J. *Traffic in Truth: Exchange between Science and Theology,* Canterbury: Canterbury Press, 2000

Poole, M. *Beliefs and Values in Science Education*, Buckingham: OUP, 1995

Southgate, C. (ed.) *God, Humanity and the Cosmos*, Edinburgh: T&T Clark, 1999

2

The Relationship between Religion and Science

If we wish to understand the interplay between science and religion today we must begin with some historical background. Part Two aims to give an account of key historical moments in the rise of science and its relationship with religion in the context and culture of its time. We will concentrate on three major landmarks: Galileo's astronomical debate with the Church in the early seventeenth century; Descartes' and Newton's mechanical world-view in the late seventeenth and eighteenth century and the search for a rational religion in the Enlightenment; Darwin's theory of evolution in the nineteenth century. The intellectual foundations of modern science were laid down in the Middle Ages, which provide the overall context of these later debates.

Galileo and his context
Galileo Galilei (1564–1642) is regarded as the 'father of modern science' as he was the first to bring together mathematics, observation and experiment, thus laying the foundations for modern physics. Galileo challenged the long-standing picture of the universe, based on the teaching of the Catholic Church and on Greek philosophy, which was taken for granted in the

Middle Ages. The Galileo affair, his celebrated confrontation with the Church, signalled the beginnings of science as an autonomous discipline and its gradual separation from religion and philosophy. The age of science is the period that came in the wake of the breakdown of the medieval world-view in the sixteenth century. We must first outline this medieval view of the cosmos, which dominated Western religious thinking prior to the rise of science, the essential background to understanding Galileo and his project.

Background of the medieval world
The Middle Ages were an age of faith, a great synthesis based on God, the self and the world related in a unified and harmonious vision. God dominated all spheres of life operating through the institution of the Catholic Church. Scholarship and knowledge were the province of the monasteries and the great universities such as Oxford and Paris founded from them. Art and architecture spoke only of religious realities; medieval cathedrals were prayers in stone pointing to the heavens, the dwelling place of God. They were also monuments to the Church's power, great building projects which demanded vast resources of men and materials. Medieval Christian culture based its world-view on two sources: firstly, the Church's interpretation of Christian revelation based on the authority of Bible. The Church revered the Bible as the inspired word of God, interpreting it literally and treating it as a repository of scientific as well as religious knowledge.

The writings of the pagan philosophers of antiquity, in particular the philosophy of Aristotle (384–322) provided the second source. Historians point out that the impact of Aristotle's thought on the later Middle Ages cannot be overestimated. For about four hundred and fifty years, from 1200 to 1650 the universities of Western Europe taught a philosophical and scientific curriculum based on the works of Aristotle. These disciplines were an essential prerequisite for studying theology.

The Medieval universities were of major importance in the development of the natural sciences. Courses in logic, metaphysics, natural philosophy, arithmetic, geometry and astronomy were prescribed. Though a pagan philosopher, Aristotle's cosmology appeared to fit neatly with the Bible's view, and their marriage produced a unified vision: the cosmos is divinely ordered and hierarchically structured. The natural world is a great 'chain of being' stretching from the highest, God the creator who is Spirit, to the lowest creation, inert matter. In this purposeful universe God draws all things to their own perfection, depending on their place in the hierarchy of beings. The human being has a very important intermediate location, being a composite of matter and spirit, above the animals and below the angels. Humans were made in the image and likeness of God; they had a unique destiny, union with God in heaven. Even so it was a not a universe centred on humans, as the creation does not exist for humans alone. Creation was a mirror in which people could, with effort, begin to discern the mind of its maker.

Knowledge advanced, not by means of hands-on experience of the world, but by way of commentaries on texts, both sacred and secular, the fruits of contemplation and reflection. St Thomas Aquinas (1225–1274) created a great synthesis of faith and reason, Christian theology and Aristotelian philosophy. He argued that philosophy (human reason) and theology (divine revelation) are compatible roads to truth. They cannot be in conflict since God, the author of all truth, gives both revelation and our capacity to reason. That does not mean they were equal. Theology, as reflection on the revealed word of God had a dominant role, the 'queen of the sciences', and philosophy was the handmaid of theology. As regards science in the Middle Ages, here too theology was the dominant partner. Science too was the handmaid of theology and compatible with it. Science provided knowledge of the natural world and so enabled people to know more about the God who created that world. It was not pursued for its own sake but only as an aid to interpreting the Bible and for defending the faith. Much of Aristotle's view of the cosmos and his theory of motion became part of the Christian world-view and over time Christianity and Aristotelian ideas appeared inseparable. Ultimately Aristotelian ideas would prove to be a hindrance to the rise of science, as would Christian teaching based on an uncritical acceptance of Aristotle's world-view. Beginning with Copernicus and Galileo, a radically new conception of the cosmos and the natural world emerged. As background to these events we need to look more closely at the scientific explorations of Aristotle and his legacy to the Medievals.

The Aristotelian world-view

Aristotle furnished the Church in the Middle Ages with its conception of the structure and operation of the physical world. Aristotle's 'natural philosophy', his division of the cosmos, theory of motion, the four elements, and the four causes provided a persuasive conceptual framework within which to experience, understand and talk about the world. We shall look at these in turn.

Aristotle divided the great sphere of the cosmos into two distinct regions, the earth ('sublunary') and the heavens ('superlunary'). They were made of entirely different stuff and operated according to different principles. Below the moon was the terrestrial region formed out of the four elements, from the heaviest to the lightest: earth, water, air and fire. The earth was imperfect, changeable, subject to growth and decay, a region where nothing ever lasts. Aristotle believed the earth was a sphere, because of the circular shadow cast by the earth during a lunar eclipse. This earth is fixed and stationary, the heavy, impure and most sluggish sphere, whose weight had caused it to sink to the centre of the universe. The earth is imperfect and its 'natural' state is to be still, at rest in the centre because rest is the natural state of all bodies composed of the four elements. Above the moon were the heavenly spheres to which the fixed stars, the sun and the seven known planets were attached. This superlunary region, composed of a pure, perfect element called 'ether' or 'quintessence' (fifth element) by Aristotle, was characterised by unchanging perfection and uniform circular motion. The sun, moon, and planets, attached to their crystalline spheres of perfect and invisible ether, moved in perfect concentric circles around the earth and at a uniform speed. The earth is at rest (geostatic) and the heavenly bodies are in perfect motion around it (geocentric). The universe has finite boundaries, the outermost sphere containing the fixed stars, beyond which was the realm of God the 'Prime Mover', the 'spiritual motor' keeping everything moving in the heavens.

Aristotle taught that a complete understanding of anything consists in answering four fundamental questions about it, expressed in his 'Four Causes'. First, there is the 'efficient cause', or the agent which brings something into existence. Second, there is the 'material cause' or the stuff that makes up a thing. Third, there is the 'formal cause', the form, the essence or 'whatness' into which the agent shapes the material cause. Fourth, there is the 'final cause', the end or purpose or goal for which it exists or towards which it tends. Let us look at an example, the making of a statue. The material cause is the stone block, the efficient cause is the sculptor who shapes the stone, the formal cause is the shape given by him/her, the final cause is the purpose or goal of the sculptor in making it, such as celebrating the life of a hero or in praise of a god. Cosmology was a search for all four causes in the universe, but by far the most important was the final cause, the Latin *finis*, meaning the goal or end or purpose. In Aristotelian science there can be no comprehensive understanding without knowing final causes. Aristotle's 'teleology', from the Greek *telos*, also meaning the goal or end, suggested an orderly and organised world, a world of purpose in which things develop toward ends determined by their natures. His primary goal was to understand the 'essential natures' of things. By discovering purpose you can deduce why a thing is the way it is. An acorn becomes an oak tree because that is its nature, the end toward which it is moving. A purposeful universe, proved to be a crucial concept for medieval philosophy and theology in the Middle Ages.

The medievals modified the geocentric view, taking into account the cosmology of Claudius Ptolemy (2nd century CE) which fitted in well with the physics of Aristotle. A geocentric universe, with planets in their glassy spheres moving at uniform speed in perfect circular orbits, did not always fit well with observation. At times planets appeared to be moving at different speeds, sometimes stationary, or even to move backwards in their orbits. To 'save the appearances', to make the facts fit the theory, Ptolemy postulated an ingenious system of 'epicycles', circles upon circles, which would account for the apparent looping backwards and forwards of the planets as they orbit the earth. Christian scholars fine-tuned the Aristotelian and Ptolemaic cosmology to bring it into line with the Bible's teaching on a purposeful creation. Certain biblical passages appeared to confirm the fixity of the earth and the mobility of the sun. For Christians, the earth was central for another reason, as the stage where the cosmic drama of salvation was being played out. Aristotle's teleology led the medievals to see that a purposeful world had a final cause who is God, not only the ground but also the end of all things. For Christians, the idea of God as Final Cause affirmed that everything had its place and purpose in God's plan. The combination provided a persuasive and aesthetically satisfying account of the world as an ordered and purposeful creation. This conceptual framework, a composite of Aristotle and Christian thought had great explanatory power. So persuasive was this model that it remained more or less unchanged and unchallenged for 1300 years, successfully answering all questions put to it.

The beginnings of science: the copernican revolution
The modern age of science began when Nicholas Copernicus, a Polish priest and mathematician, published *On the Revolution of the Heavenly Spheres* in 1543. His principal thesis stated that

the earth is a planet revolving around a motionless central sun. Copernicus suggested a sun-centred (heliocentric) universe; the sun is the fixed and immobile (heliostatic) centre around which the earth and the other planets revolve. He claimed there were two great movements of the earth: rotating on its axis once a day and revolving around the sun once a year. His reasons for a sun-centred universe were partly mystical, partly mathematical. He considered that it was more fitting that the 'lamp of the universe' should light up everything from the centre. Ptolemy's geocentric universe, with more and more epicycles being added to fit observations, was in danger of collapsing under its own complex weight. For Copernicus it was mathematically simpler and more elegant to see the sun at the centre, eliminating some but not all of the anomalies of Ptolemy. The Copernican Revolution marked a radical change in understanding from the older geostatic view. Copernicus was reluctant to publish, until the year of his death, as he feared the ridicule of the Aristotelian academics, for whom the geocentric view was self-evidently true. Copernicus based his view of the earth, as rotating on its axis and revolving about the sun, on an inferior discipline, mathematics. This claim was contradicted by the higher discipline of physics; a fundamental dictum of Aristotelian physics stated that a simple body (earth) could only have one motion proper to it. Furthermore, a heliocentric universe appeared to conflict with the Bible, with a literal interpretation of some Old Testament passages, which suggested geocentricism.

What followed was a 'paradigm shift', a crisis in the developing scientific community in which two radically different and irreconcilable views were in competition. An acute and hapless complication resulted from the Church's backing of the geostatic view: defending Christianity and defending Aristotle became coupled in a way that brought Christianity into unnecessary conflict with the new sciences; an attack on Aristotle appeared to be an attack on Christianity itself. The crisis came to a head with the arrival of Galileo, who vigorously defended the new Copernican model.

Galileo and the new astronomy

Care must be taken in attempting to outline the essentials of the Galileo affair to avoid a caricature of a complex historical situation; the debate down the centuries has often been used for propaganda purposes, as the litmus test for the essential incompatibility between science and religion. Galileo was Professor of Mathematics at the University of Padua, working on the physics of motion and interested in the new science of astronomy. In 1609 he used the telescope for the first time as a scientific instrument to study the heavens. Looking through the telescope he made discoveries, which were to shake the foundations of the Aristotelian view of the cosmos. He saw that the moon was not a perfectly smooth sphere, but pockmarked with mountains and valleys like the earth. Hence the earth was not unique, but a moving planet like the others. Jupiter had four satellites or moons orbiting it; no longer could one hold that heavenly bodies revolve exclusively around the earth. He observed phases in Venus, like the moon has for us, the only explanation for which was that Venus moves around the sun and not the earth. He was 'overwhelmed by the vast quantity of stars' in the Milky Way which could not be enlarged by a telescope and so must be vast distances away beyond the planets. His results, published in 1610 in *The Starry Messenger*, revolutionised astronomy and laid the foundations of the modern science of motion.

Galileo's fame grew and he was appointed Chief Mathematician and Philosopher to the Grand Duke of Tuscany. His observations and measurements fatally undermined the ancient Aristotelian world-view. Reactions were mixed, ranging from great enthusiasm to outright rejection. Many acclaimed Galileo as the new Columbus discovering new worlds. Academic philosophers in the universities were extremely hostile, some deriding the telescope as revealing only smudges and optical defects on the lens! The Church was initially sympathetic and the Pope Paul V warmly welcomed Galileo. But it was also cautious, as it feared some of the implications of a heliocentric universe for Christian teaching. The Jesuit astronomers of the Roman College agreed with Galileo that Ptolemy and Aristotle were undermined, but not necessarily that Copernicus was right. Galileo's observations and discoveries could be accommodated equally well by an alternative theory of Tycho Brahe (1546–1601), the Danish astronomer. He proposed a complicated model of the earth at the centre with the sun and moon orbiting it, but all other planets circled the sun. This theory fitted better with the Bible, so the Church encouraged an open debate about opposing views.

Galileo was challenged to produce evidence that Copernicus was right; a convincing Aristotelian 'true demonstration', going back to necessary causes in a deductive argument, was impossible. Moreover, there could be no planetary observation by which people on the earth can prove that the earth is moving in an orbit around the sun. So all Galileo's observations with the telescope could be just as easily accounted for by the theory of Tycho Brahe. Notwithstanding these difficulties, Galileo crusaded aggressively for the Copernican view in his *Letter on Sunspots* 1613, dismissing and ridiculing all opposition. He insisted, despite the discoveries of Johann Kepler (1571–1630) that planetary orbits are elliptical, that the planets orbit the sun in perfect circles. He claimed to have evidence that the earth moved, incorrectly reasoning that the earth's motion caused the tides; Kepler correctly argued it was the moon's attraction.

In 1616 the Holy Office of the Catholic Church declared the claim that the earth moves around the sun and the sun is motionless in the centre is contrary to Holy Scripture and should not be defended. The Bible, then interpreted literally, supported the geocentric view in passages such as Joshua 10:13; the sun is moving but stands still only by the mighty action of God. Psalms 92 and 103 speak of a stationary earth. Galileo was officially warned by his friend Cardinal Bellarmine not to teach Copernicanism as a fact, that is, as a realist physical theory about how things truly are, but to treat it as a hypothesis, that is, as a useful calculating device, a mathematical theory. The Church had no difficulty with the Copernican theory as a speculative hypothesis confined to mathematical astronomy; that did not conflict with the traditional view, which described how things actually are. Bellarmine told Galileo that if a true demonstration for the movement of the earth could be found, then the Church would have to abandon its traditional, literal reading of all passages that were contrary. Galileo proceeded cautiously until 1632 when he published his *Dialogue of the Two Chief World Systems*. Here he compared Copernicus' view with the traditional one based on Aristotle and Ptolemy. He strongly defended the Copernican system as a physical theory about the actual universe. Furthermore, Galileo lampooned the Aristotelian world-view and insulted his erstwhile friend Cardinal Barberini, now Pope Urban VIII, by sketching him as a 'simpleton', one of the 'mental pygmies', supporters of Aristotle.

Galileo was summoned before the Holy Office in 1633 and accused of breaking his promise of 1616 'not to hold, teach or defend' the Copernican view. He was condemned 'on suspicion of heresy', and threatened with imprisonment and torture. Galileo denied holding Copernican views four times under oath, an obvious untruth which risked conviction for perjury. He challenged the literal interpretation of Scripture and the authority of the Catholic Church; he was compelled to recant Copernicanism and to keep silent on the subject and was placed under house arrest in his own home in Florence until his death in 1642.

Galileo and the Church
The Galileo debate is a classic case of the need to understand the wider cultural context, the social, religious and spiritual climate of his times, which underpinned his dispute with the Church. It

is important to tease out the issues that led to these conclusions. Galileo was very religious and wished no quarrel with his Catholic faith; he was anxious to relate his discoveries about the world to his Christian understanding. So he tried hard to resolve the apparent contradiction between Copernican astronomy and the Bible. For Galileo, the hermeneutical question took centre stage: how should the Bible be read and how should that reading affect or be affected by science? The question concerned the legitimate authority of the Bible and its limits: did the Bible teach Aristotelian cosmology as a matter of faith or accept it *de facto*? Galileo was certain it was the latter, that Christianity had taken for granted the Aristotelian view and both had become confused. An attack on Aristotle should not be seen as an attack on the Bible. Galileo's approach was firstly, to attempt to separate biblical teaching from the geocentric view and secondly, to show that the interpretation of the Bible should not go against established views in science.

The 'Two Books Metaphor'
In 1615, his *Letter to Grand Duchess Christina* tried to show the compatibility between the Bible and the Copernican view. He espoused the 'two books metaphor' first proposed by Francis Bacon: God reveals himself in two great complementary books, the book of the Bible and the book of Nature. He cautioned that it is mistake to confuse the two: the Church should not lock in changing astronomical theories to biblical texts, since the theories may turn out to be false; this 'sanctified science' could only undermine the authority of the Bible. The Bible is not a scientific treatise: much of the language in it is figurative, so the terms that imply a stationary earth and a moving sun are not literal scientific descriptions. The Bible is intended to teach 'not how the heavens go but how one goes to heaven'; that is, it teaches moral and spiritual truths necessary for our salvation. The Book of Nature, 'how the heavens go', is concerned with the natural world, God's creation, and is written in the language

of mathematics. So in evaluating the Copernican view, mathematical criteria are more important than what the Bible has to say. The truths of science and the truths of religion cannot contradict one another, because God is the author of all truth; so, if there is a contradiction it must be the result of a mistaken interpretation. There is room for both science and religion if we recognise the limitations of each.

The Church reacted negatively to a layman daring to challenge the traditional supremacy of theology by his own personal interpretation of the Bible. The Church was highly sensitive at this time to the question, who was authorised to interpret the Bible? In a time of religious upheaval, the Reformation and the Thirty Years War, the Catholic Church had become extremely defensive at the erosion of her religious and political power. The Reformers had challenged the authority of Church teaching by appealing to scripture alone (*sola scriptura*) and encouraged individual interpretation of the Bible. The Council of Trent decreed that the ultimate authority to interpret the Bible belonged to the Church Fathers and to Church Tradition going back to the Apostles. Galileo was presuming to interpret the Bible by himself and so was acting like a Reformer. Galileo's argumentative personality, his personal attacks, his ridiculing of all who would not accept his arguments, some of which were plainly wrong, did not help his cause. He made outlandish claims that he alone had discovered everything new in the sky! Known as a 'wrangler', he had an unhappy knack of making enemies of staunch friends in the Church who were sympathetic to his cause.

The Aristotelian geocentric view could not be shifted overnight, not only because of Church support, but because it was central to the Medieval cultural mind-set and to human imagination from Dante to Milton and Shakespeare. A radical, grand new idea needed time to be accepted; as things stood, Galileo could not prove Copernicus to be true and many of his details were inaccurate. Science had no status; there was no community of peers like an Academy of Sciences to settle disputes between rival theories. Theology still claimed supremacy in all matters, including science. When the medieval person looked at the stars and planets, set in their crystalline spheres, he or she saw meaning and significance because the earth was the centre of the universe and human life was the special object of God's care. To abandon a geocentric and embrace a heliocentric universe would involve rethinking the Church's traditional interpretation of the Bible and would have many unacceptable, if not frightening, theological consequences. If the earth is not unique, then humans are not unique, and then maybe the coming of God's Son in the incarnation is not unique? Then there is the question of the location of heaven and hell: a moving imperfect earth, with hell at its core, contaminates the perfect heavens putting human destiny in doubt. The psychological impact of the Copernican universe of vast distances and huge space reinforced the feeling of being lost and adrift in a shoreless sea. The poet John Donne summed up the reaction to the new universe, 'tis all in pieces; all coherence gone'.

The beginnings of modern science

The Galileo affair marked the breakdown of the medieval universe and the beginnings of modern science. Galileo laid the foundations for a whole new cosmology and a new physics of motion:

a. Galileo's great contribution was to scientific method: his genius was to combine mathematical reasoning with empirical observation and experiment, the bedrock of modern science. By 'thought experiments' he meant a constant interaction between mathematical abstractions and the concrete world of our experience, between theoretical ideas and experimental data. Nature was not mystical, but particles of matter in motion, and mathematics were the key to understanding it; the physical world revealed basic properties that can be measured. The application of mathematical methods to the physical world is the single most significant change to the ancient world-view in the seventeenth century. Galileo's formulation of the law of falling bodies began a progressive and increasingly successful description of the world using the tool of mathematics. Galileo was able to demonstrate that a projectile follows the path of a parabola with two independent motions: a uniform, forward horizontal motion and an accelerated, downward or vertical motion.

b. Galileo's inductive method undermined the deductive method of Aristotle. Galileo struggled against a background of religious authority that gave Greek notions of perfection priority over observation and experimental evidence. Medieval thought was deductive – it deduced what should happen from universal first principles, in contrast to the later inductive method of arriving at a theory from observation. Deduction meant starting from the most general principles, moving to the more particular and concrete, from the top down. Inductive meant beginning with concrete data, moving to more general patterns and hypotheses to explain the data, from the bottom up. Aristotle's universe, divided into an imperfect, changing earth and a perfect, unchanging heavenly region, was based on the way things must necessarily be as they flow from the most general principles, the way theorems flow from the axioms of Euclid. The shape of the world must be a perfect sphere, and perfect motion must then be circular; it follows that in the perfect heavens, the planets in their perfect spheres have circular and uniform motion. The earth is imperfect and its 'natural' state is to be still, at rest in the centre because rest is the natural state of all bodies composed of the four elements. Galileo's telescope was the instrument that punctured this deductive vision and showed it to be flawed. For Galileo the structure of the physical world cannot be deduced in an ivory tower from first principles; observation, measurement and experimentation can only discover how it works. Appeal to authorities, however venerable, was no substitute for the hands-on investigation of the physical world. The way things must be and the way things actually are may be very different.

c. Galileo's understanding of motion undermined Aristotle's physics of 'common sense'. Galileo made his greatest contribution to the content of science in his *Discourses Concerning Two New Sciences* towards the end of his life, establishing laws governing bodies in motion, and founding the new science of dynamics. Aristotle's physics of 'common sense' appeared eminently reasonable to the Middle Ages: it is 'obvious' to the observer that the sun moves from east to west and the earth is still; commonsense suggests that the earth does not spin on its axis. Aristotle dismissed the contention of a spinning earth by 'commonsense' arguments: the arrow fired vertically into the air lands at the feet of the archer; besides, there would be a constant wind and birds would be blown off trees if the earth were to spin! Aristotle's 'experiments' settle nothing about a rotating earth: the results would be the same whether the earth spins or not. Aristotle answered the question why a stone falls to earth in terms of purpose or goal; everything is pulled into the centre of the universe by a mystical impulse, it returns to its 'natural' place of rest as a heavy element. Galileo asked not why objects fall (*telos* or goal), but *how* they fall. This was a crucial move away from explanations in terms of mystical purposes in matter to mechanical causes; there are forces and masses at work rather than a hierarchy of purposes. He endeavoured to discover the laws governing motion and these could only be detected by reasoning and not by our senses. The approach of Galileo also illustrates the counterintuitive nature of science, against common sense.

What appears to our senses to be the case may not necessarily be the case, like a stick that appears bent in water.

There were other factors that influenced the rise of science that had nothing explicitly to do with religion. The great humanistic movement of the Renaissance directed attention to secular subjects, to the study of the natural and the human for their own sakes. The growth of trade, the developments of crafts and commerce all demanded more precise instruments and measurement. Military technology required more accurate calibration of the engines of war. Galileo's work on the motion of projectiles was useful to improving the accuracy of guns and cannons. Measurement and more accurate calibration could have technological applications.

Science and the reaction of religions

An unfortunate consequence of the condemnation of Galileo was its use to reinforce the myth of an incompatibility between religion and science. The inability to distinguish between religion and science in the Middle Ages made Galileo's ideas unacceptable to believers of his time. He fought on two fronts, firstly against the authority of Aristotle and the geocentric view; and, secondly, the Church authorities in their literal interpretation of the Bible. Both forces combined to have him condemned. The Galileo story was later retold portraying Galileo as the man of reason and enlightenment, thwarted by ignorant, reactionary and superstitious churchmen, intent on preventing progress. Galileo had tried unsuccessfully to distinguish between Christian faith and the philosophies – from Aristotle to Ptolemy – through which it was expressed. The 'Two Books' of nature and scripture should be seen as separate but complementary. His rejection of a biblical literalism, that the Bible was a book of scientific information, rather than revelation about God's salvation, strikes us as a very modern view.

Relations between Christianity and science became more intricate as the seventeenth century progressed. In the aftermath of Galileo, the study of a heliocentric universe could no longer be pursued as vigorously within Catholic countries as in Protestant lands. For Galileo, the Catholic Church had made a disastrous mistake, which was to have long-term consequences, by taking an official position for one kind of science as against another. Nevertheless, by the middle of the century French Catholics like Rene Descartes and Pierre Gassendi were among the chief contributors to the mechanical view of the universe.

After the Reformation, Protestants had greater freedom to study the Bible and to trust in individual reason rather than relying on authorities. These factors gave the discussion on religion and science a social, political and religious edge. The vigorous defence of the traditional geocentric view by the Catholic Church was also motivated by the desire for order and stability in a world that appeared to be degenerating into free-thinking anarchy. However, the Reformers too condemned the new scientific findings. Martin Luther and Melanchthon vehemently condemned Copernicus' view as contrary to the Scriptures and the Lutheran Johann Kepler was once forced to take refuge with the Jesuits to escape persecution. The Calvinist work ethic appears to have particularly supported science; it was the duty of the good Christian to discover the wisdom of God in his works. In the Royal Society, the oldest academy for the promotion of the sciences, seven out of ten members were Puritans and some were clergy. Scientists of all hues were motivated in their science by religious reasons, that in doing their work they were 'thinking God's thoughts after him'.

2.2   DESCARTES AND NEWTON: SCIENCE VERSUS RELIGION

The seventeenth and eighteenth centuries saw the increasing secularisation of knowledge following the success of the new scientific method; yet, it was impossible to understand the world without God. The world was measurable and analysable, but it was still a divinely created world. The workings of the world could be increasingly described by natural causes, but it was also the place of God's providence. By the seventeenth century Copernican astronomy was widely accepted. The scientific evidence was by then secure and the Biblical passages that seemed to conflict with it were given a non-literal interpretation in most Catholic and Protestant circles.

But the eighteenth century witnessed the gradual unravelling of the close interaction between Christianity and science. Rene Descartes undermined the Aristotelian world through his dualism of subject and object and Isaac Newton's physics reinforced this view of a mechanistic world determined by laws, the human being an exception. Both Descartes and Newton had a place for God in their scheme of things; they accepted the two books metaphor. But the consequence of their science was to remove God from a mechanical universe. Yet, their approaches and methods could not be more different. Descartes was a rationalist philosopher whereas Newton was an empirical scientist.

Descartes and his influence

Rene Descartes (1596–1650), considered the founder of modern philosophy, used the method of systematic doubt in order to establish what could be known for certain. His approach was known as rationalism, seeing the mind, rather than the senses, as the starting point for certain knowledge. By the use of reasoning human beings can discover truths that are universal and necessary. Rationalism sometimes appeals to 'innate ideas', ideas that seem to be naturally implanted within the mind. Much of what passed for knowledge in the Middle Ages depended on commentaries on ancient books and learning was in the hands of Church authorities. The split of the Reformation undermined the authority of the churches raising questions about how religious truth could now be found. Descartes lived in an age of scepticism; there were conflicting claims and no reliable method of putting knowledge on a firm foundation, freed from dubious traditions and opinions based on appeal to historical authorities. Perhaps human reason could prevail where religious traditions and authorities had failed. All interpretations of the natural world would have to submit to the bar of reason. Descartes' aim was to lay the foundations of certain knowledge, to establish that scientific knowledge was possible.

The significance of Descartes' Cogito

Descartes began his enterprise with his Method of Doubt. Since he was looking for certainty, he laid aside anything in which he could find the slightest doubt. He doubted all empirical evidence, since our senses often deceive us. He could doubt the existence of the external world outside his mind as, like a dream, it may only be in his head. Further, he supposed, if there were a 'malign spirit' trying to deceive him about everything, was there anything this spirit could not mislead him about? Descartes thought there was one bedrock certainty: his only certain knowledge was of himself as a thinking being, since to deny it would be a contradiction: 'Cogito ergo sum, I think therefore I am'. Even if he has a false thought, it is still a thought he is thinking; he is consciously aware and therefore he knows he must exist. Descartes' systematic doubt had swept away everything so now he attempted to reconstruct the world on a firm foundation starting with the one certainty of the 'cogito'. He had to find something in the content of his consciousness that leads outside himself – that was the idea of God. The criterion of truth was the clarity and distinctness of an idea. Of all ideas, the clearest was the idea of God, because it was not derived from the experience of the senses and could not have been invented by human imagination. The idea of God is unique, the idea of an infinite being could not have come from finite creatures like himself; the greater cannot come from the lesser. God could only have planted it in his mind himself; since he has this idea of God, it could only be because there actually exists a God, corresponding to his idea, who created him. Since God is benevolent and trustworthy, he is the guarantor that Descartes' conviction about the existence of the external world is not mistaken. God helped to put the world back again, but in the aftermath of systematic doubt it was a radically reconstructed world.

The world consisted of two different sorts of entity: there is the external world, given to me by God, and there is also me, observing the external world. Descartes made a radical distinction between the *'res cogitans'* and the *'res extensa'*, between the thinking subject, the inner domain of spirit, and the outer world, the extended world of matter. Cartesian dualism split mind and matter, subject and object, observer and observed. The real human is a thinking being with interiority and freedom, but linked to a physical body, part of the predictable physical universe, which is not essential to the immaterial thinking mind. What kept these radically different 'things' together? God guaranteed the co-ordination of mind and body, the 'ghost in a machine'. Descartes never satisfactorily explained their interaction, how the human mind could 'push' the body around.

Cartesian dualism, in some form, got embedded in Western thought for three hundred years as it provided the impetus for a systematic scientific approach to the world. From this dualistic split, Descartes laid the philosophical foundations for a mechanical conception of the universe, totally conditioned and determined, every movement theoretically predictable. The external world is simply extension, it takes up space and can be treated by geometry and mathematics; it is what science studies. Matter is co-extensive with space, filled with particles of matter, which behave according to the laws of motion and the principle of inertia. Descartes was a rationalist in that he considered the fundamental properties of the world and of the mind could be discovered *a priori* by philosophical reflection; he denied priority to experience but not its importance. He did not believe that the whole of science could be deduced from metaphysical first principles, from purely mathematical or logical reasoning. Experimentation is essential to distinguish between some ways of explaining nature and others; different intellectual models of the world could be constructed within the fundamental laws of nature, so experiment was needed to discover which truly represents nature.

Descartes and the disappearance of God
Though God was indispensable to Descartes in arriving at his method of knowing the true nature of things, once you were in possession of the method you did not need God anymore to do science. Descartes wanted to free the process of science from all theological interference and constraints, something that had bedevilled Galileo. Yet, God was at the root of his system and he did not want his inquiry to lead to a godless world: God created the world and he guaranteed our knowledge of it. The irony was that Descartes' rational construction made it easier for God to disappear from the world and from peoples' understanding of it. He paved the way for Deism, a God who was outside the material universe and played no part in it after his initial act of creation. A spiritual God no longer intervened in the spiritless and godless world of material motion. From Descartes on, the book of nature referred just to itself. Descartes' God is removed from the material universe that is self-sufficient and self-acting. Nature could no longer be seen as the Book that reveals God. For some thinkers of the later Enlightenment, Deism in turn paved the way for atheism, the denial of the existence of God. What difference did God make if he was an absent God with no role in the world? The logical conclusion of an absent God was a non-existent God. Paradoxically, in Descartes' use of philosophy and in Newton's use of science to secure God's place in the world, both contributed to the rise of Deism in the eighteenth century and eventually to the rise of atheism. The implications are discussed in the section on the Enlightenment.

The human subject, already demoted from the centre of things in a heliocentric world, was also now alienated from the material universe by Descartes; nevertheless, the mind and its power of reason were an exception to the inhospitable material world. Rationalism provided the scientists of the seventeenth century with a powerful tool to subject competing interpretations of nature to the scrutiny of reason. Newton represented the most successful adaptation of science, with his accent on experimentation, to the new emphasis on the universal truths of reason.

Newton and the mathematical paradigm

Isaac Newton (1642–1727), the founder of classical physics, brought to further realisation the scientific revolution, the alliance of mathematics and experimentation begun by Galileo. The interaction of theory and experiment was even more intense in Newton. He established mathematics as the basic language of science to describe the workings of the world, inventing integral and differential calculus and binomial theorem. Mathematics was a way of examining and manipulating abstract concepts that could help to make sense of our experience. It played a central role in Newton's science: mathematical formulae produced ways of calculating and ways of predicting. He combined this theoretical strength with the practical, dedicating himself to the empirical work of observation, measurement and experimentation. This meticulous empirical work, helped by more precise instruments for accurate calibration and measurement, proved decisive for his great discoveries in mechanics and optics. Newton's scientific method was grounded empirically in observation and the collecting of data, from which reason could construct theories or laws, expressing them in mathematical formulae. In contrast to the rationalism of Descartes, for Newton all knowledge began with experience of the world, with particular observations from which the general laws of nature could be worked out and expressed in mathematical terms. His genius lay in his ability to pull together the apparently unrelated contributions of various scientific disciplines and to unify them in a grand vision of how the universe worked. He proposed a set of theoretical concepts (gravity and the laws of motion), which was able to encompass within a single unified scheme vast reaches of data from many types of phenomena.

Newton wrote that he saw further because 'he stood on the shoulders of giants', his predecessors Copernicus, Galileo and Kepler. He noticed connections between Galileo's conclusions on earthly motion and Kepler's views on planetary motion. He first tackled the laws that governed earthly motion, giving greater precision to vague ideas that were circulating after Galileo, enunciating the three laws of motion. All motion follows fixed laws: objects continue either in rest or in uniform motion in a straight line unless acted upon by some external forces.

The critical move was his conviction that the laws that apply to earthly motion also hold good for the heavens, the motion of the planets in free space. He applied the laws of motion to the orbit of the moon around the earth; according to the first law, the law of inertia, the moon is trying to escape the earth moving in a straight line, unless acted upon by other forces. The catalyst for the unification of the two was the famous 'myth of the apple': while sitting in his garden in 1666, an apple fell on Newton's head and jolted him into a new world, the world of universal gravitation, and so classical physics was born. The force that made the apple to fall to earth was the same force that held the moon in its orbit round the earth, and the earth and the other planets around the sun. Gravity concerned the mutual attraction between bodies (masses), a constant of proportionality, which can be given a precise mathematical formula: the force of attraction gets stronger the more massive the bodies and the closer they are together. Newton's laws of motion and gravity made sense of what Galileo and others observed through instruments and the measurements they had made. The key advance of Newton was that he grasped the mathematical principles that made what they had observed coherent. Newton showed it was gravity, not some magnetic (Kepler) or mystic (Aristotle) force that bound the universe together. He showed that a vast range of observational data could be explained on the basis of a few universal principles. His grand synthesis revealed that the whole physical world could be explained in terms of three laws of motion and the law of gravity, the cornerstone of classical physics. They laid the foundations of a world-view that dominated the Western world for three hundred years. Newton's central ideas were enshrined in his celebrated book of physics *Philosophiae Naturalis Principia Mathematica* of 1687.

The natural world for Newton, therefore, though it appears complex, is ultimately simple. What is important and fundamental about natural phenomena can be described in mathematical language. This led to a distinction between primary and secondary qualities: Mass, extension in space and duration in time, belonged to the object itself, could be measured and were amenable to experimentation and mathematical analysis. Newton was able to establish precise ideas of force, velocity, momentum and acceleration on the basis of these primary qualities. Secondary qualities, such as colour, smell, temperature and texture were dismissed as subjective as they could not be measured accurately. Science attempted to reduce everything to primary qualities, as they appeared to be objective, fixed and measurable. The universe then could be thought of as a great machine acting according to fixed laws. This mechanistic world-view presented a well-ordered, stable and predictable world; the whole world was composed of moving, interacting parts that never cease, entirely determined by unchanging laws, every detail precisely predictable. Classical physics was confident that mathematics could predict the future motion of every particle in a deterministic universe if their positions, velocities and masses were known.

Newton further undermined the Aristotelian world-view: gone forever was the view that the universe is divided into earthly and heavenly regions, made of different stuff and having different motion. Furthermore, things seeking their natural purposes or ends do not explain movement on the earth; it is not natural for objects to be at rest. Newton saw that motion on the earth and in the heavens is fundamentally the same; in a dynamic universe there is no still centre around which everything revolves. The law of gravity sweeps the ceaseless motion of the universe into a grand sense of unity and wholeness. Nature is a great law-abiding machine, a structure of forces and masses rather than a hierarchy of purposes.

Newton and God

Newton was very religious, being a member of the Church of England, and was attracted to the austere piety of the Puritans. His love of the Bible, which he understood to be the literal word of God, led him to study the providential role of God in history, God's handiwork. Discipline, hard work and good habits were the virtues God demanded and he felt the need to account to God for every moment of his life. He saw the study of nature as a religious duty and he was motivated by a religious desire to trace the wisdom of God in his works of creation. The mechanical universe, then, had religious implications: a mathematically designed and ordered universe suggested a Designer; God lay behind, designed and guaranteed the mechanistic world. The world worked according to mathematical principles, but God provided these principles; there were laws of nature only because there was a divine Lawgiver. Mathematics, the clean, precise, detached and elegant language of science, unencumbered by emotion or prejudice, was the code in which the laws were written.

An Irishman, Robert Boyle, a founder member of the Royal Society in the seventeenth century, held that the universe is a machine, like the clock at Strasbourg, an intricate system of moving parts keeping perfect time. The clock is the symbol of Newton's world: it showed design, creation for a purpose and an intelligence behind it. The universe required a creator the way the clock required a clockmaker. Newton's role for God in a mechanical universe was to have profound negative effects in the later interplay between religion and science in the Enlightenment. We shall now explore the implications of his claim of a place for God within his scientific picture of the universe.

The world-machine designed by an intelligent creator, the divine mathematician who is behind the laws, preserved the distinction between creator and creation. God is transcendent, other than the world he created. Newton wanted to refute the two dangerous notions of pantheism and atheism. Pantheism sees the world as an organism, the identification of nature with God as the 'world-soul'. The Greeks understood the world as semi-divine; but such a view of the world as sacred discouraged scientific experimentation as it would seem to be like sacrilege. The clockmaker-clock analogy took God out of the natural world. Yet, Newton wanted to avoid the opposite danger, the dismissal of God from the universe altogether in atheism; God is distinct from, though he is involved with, the world in some way.

Hence, the crucial question: what place is there for God in a purely mechanical, autonomous universe that runs according to predictable laws? He tried to bridge the gap between the infinite God and the world of extended matter. With his universal law of gravity, Newton brought God into science in a very direct and startling way: God is omnipresent in the universe through the medium of absolute time and space. He believed that God, quite literally, contains the universe in himself. God provides the infinite boundary, the box or container in which finite created matter had its being. The material universe is in constant motion, but God provides the fixed frame within which the laws of motion are at work. He is at rest, stable and unchanging outside the universe, on whom the moving parts depend. Newton's God is not at the centre but outside, holding the whole dynamic system within a timeless, motionless framework. How? Through the immaterial force of gravity. The planets are revolving in free space ruled only by the force of gravity, the glue that holds the universe together. God's 'face shines' in the mysterious force of gravity; God sustains the world and acts upon it, from outside it, through the force of gravity. Nature is a coded witness to the creator; it does not speak directly of God, as it is dark and empty of meaning, yet for those who understand the mathematics it contains a hidden message. The universe would be unintelligible except in terms of a wise and holy God whose rational design could be discerned in what he had made.

Newton was worried that his mechanical universe drastically reduced God's activity in the world and could be interpreted as Deism, and might lead ultimately to atheism. God was a distant, controlling force acting through the laws. He envisaged God sometimes acting more directly in the universe: he had also had a continuing function in adjusting the solar system. God occasionally corrected the irregularities in the motion of the planets by means of the 'divine arm', keeping the mechanism of the universe in good working order. He also had a second duty in preventing the stars from colliding, as the force of gravity would clump the stars together in a static universe. God is not only the creator but also the repairer of the universe.

Newton's mechanical paradigm had an enormous impact in the wider social and cultural context of the early eighteenth century, demonstrating that science does not exist in a vacuum. Newton's *Principia* was greeted with almost religious enthusiasm; scientific reason would provide the new unifying principle. Reason and science would be the new way to God, a more secure way than appeals to the Bible and tradition, whose authority had been challenged. The new science might fill the gap left by the fragmentation of religious authority. The all-embracing theory of gravity satisfied a deep religious need for order and stability in the cosmos. God, the principle of order was, in spite of the problems with the Churches, in charge of the universe after all, the guarantor of harmony and mobility.

In summary, Newton's clockwork universe required a clockmaker-God to create it, to hold it in place and to run it. The thrust of his defence of God's relation with the universe, his natural theology, was to argue from a designed, regular universe to its intelligent Designer.

Science and religion in the Enlightenment

During the eighteenth century philosophies developed in the European Continent and in Britain that reflected the new spirit, the individual human as perfectible by reason, generally known as the Enlightenment. Nature could be understood and tamed through science and technology, the practical application of science. New instruments were devised, like the microscope and the barometer, giving more accurate measurements of the physical world. Technological developments like the steam engine, balloon flight and gas lighting, acted as proof in the popular mind that science must be good and right, because of the practical benefits it delivered. The Enlightenment challenged the authority of great institutions like the Churches, which had a monopoly on knowledge: authority was no longer to reside in Bible or Church but in the reason and conscience of the individual inquirer. A great shift in self-understanding had taken place since the Middle Ages: the world was no longer a place dominated by spiritual forces, influenced by the planetary spheres, with things acting according to final causes. After Newton and Descartes, the world was a predictable, rational place, a giant mechanism established by the creator, who was a distant controlling force.

The growth of a rational religion

The spirit of the times reflected the great optimism that reason and science would prove to be, where ancient authorities had failed, the new way to God. For Descartes and Newton, the universe is unintelligible except in terms of a wise and holy God whose rational design could be seen in what he had made. The 'Two Books' of the Bible and nature were separate but complementary: the study of nature as the book of God's works, complementing that of his words, his revelation in the Bible. The authority of revealed religion based on the Bible was increasingly seen to be vulnerable to criticism. The Enlightenment spirit became hostile to supernatural revelation and the conflicting beliefs of the various Churches. The Western conscience found itself deeply scandalised by the endless dogmatic disputes concerning the Bible, the sectarian divisions and fratricidal wars that undermined the moral and religious truth-claims of the Churches. The Churches were part of the problem as they unintentionally provided a fertile ground for atheism, the denial of God. It was imperative that the existence and the meaning of God should be established independently of any Church, historical religion, or appeal to the Bible. Newton had shown that nature provided the book that everyone can read, irrespective of one's religious allegiance. He saw God's hand in the harmonious design of the universe and in the laws as an expression of God's purposes and sovereignty. Optimism about the power of reason led some thinkers to claim that a 'natural religion' underpins all religions, it is foundational to all confessions containing their essential truths, and can be discovered by reason. There were three stages in the development of this natural or rational religion:

1. *The two books together:* At first, claims about divine revelation through the Bible and Church tradition were not discounted; they were used to show that Christianity was a rational, orderly religion, whose dictates could be read off the face of nature. Natural theology, the argument from design, could support revealed theology, the message of the Bible. This was the position of Newton, Descartes and other Christian thinkers who saw no contradiction between their science and their faith; on the contrary, they tried to defend the truths of faith by means

of reason and science. Some religious groups saw religion and science as entirely different spheres and saw no need to argue from one to the other. They focused on the personal and emotional aspects of religion and were unconcerned with the new mechanical view of the universe; they were wary of Deism and the minimalist God of rational religion. These included the Methodists in England and the Pietists in Germany.

2. The Book of Nature alone: The rise of deism: The second stage commenced with the claim by some thinkers that rational religion replaced revelation. The eighteenth century saw a great flourishing of natural theology: Newton's mechanics had revealed how the Creator Designer had worked and was working in the natural world. What truths could a rational and universal religion uncover? There were three certain, universal truths: a Supreme Being, the immortality of the soul, and moral obligation. It was through the rational study of nature that God's attributes could be inferred and from the study of human nature that the status and destiny of human beings could be discovered. This universal religion is available at all times and in every place. The design argument enabled eighteenth-century rationalists to have a place for religion, but only at the expense of an impoverished view of God. Exclusive concentration on the Book of Nature tended to lose the connection to the richness of the Biblical God who reaches out in a saving way to people in history.

Newton's regular mechanical universe opened the way for 'Deism'. His system both affirmed God and limited what God could be. God was outside the cosmos, setting the initial conditions and keeping the mechanism in good working order. But if God made the machine perfect, then there would be no need for God to intervene in a miraculous way, as Newton claimed he did. God was progressively being edged out of descriptions of the workings of the physical world in favour of purely natural and physical explanations. Newton imported

God into his science to fill what turned out to be gaps in the scientific knowledge of his time. Later, Laplace showed that the irregularities of planetary orbits would automatically cancel each other out over a long time-span. Newton had claimed that God stepped in to correct them. The 'God-of-the-Gaps', that God explains the gaps in our knowledge, proved vulnerable to criticism; the more science developed and filled the gaps, the less God was required to explain anything. God becomes redundant as a scientific explanation, as Laplace claimed 'he had no need of the God hypothesis'.

For the eighteenth-century deists nature is a closed system, determined by the laws of matter in motion. David Hume (1711–1776) undermined the Design argument, that design did not require a religious explanation to understand what was observed as it could be the product of chance. All theological ideas were excluded so there was no possibility of revelation or intervention or miracle. God did not interact with the world; he had no personal involvement with or special place within creation. Belief in an external clockmaker God, who created the world in the beginning but then left it to its own devices and was no longer active in it, was known as Deism. God put the laws in place and they demonstrate the wisdom of God. What started as an attempt to reinterpret God in nature, from within the Christian community rooted in the Bible, ended with a distant and impersonal God. The question inevitably arose whether such an impoverished God could be eliminated completely from the mechanical world-view; there was no further need for such a God

3. *From deism to atheism:* For many, Deism was the slippery slope that could lead to atheism, to the absolute rejection of God. The battle between deists and atheists lay in the interpretation of nature: nature as the work of a providential Creator or the product of blind mechanical forces. The clockmaker God was external to the workings of the cosmos as a perfect clock, once

wound up, would not need the clockmaker. Deism exaggerated the remoteness of God at the expense of his presence and involvement with the world. The deists credited so little activity to God that their view virtually amounted to atheism: a God who no longer played an active role in the world was a dead God. An utterly transcendent God, who was not immanent in his creation, was of no earthly use and became surplus to requirements. French philosophers of the Enlightenment developed a strong hostility to the Church and heralded the triumph of science over the superstition of religion, espousing a materialist world-view. A militant atheism was advanced in the name of science: God was neither in the revelations of the Churches nor hidden in the forces of nature.

The core issue of the Enlightenment religion and science debate lay in the inadequate conception of God that natural religion attempted to defend. Deism was subsequently found to be wanting by many Christians because it made God external to the universe, rather than being immanent, bound up with what happened within it. There was an assumption that if the idea of the world as a purposely designed mechanism, pointing to a divine Designer, was overturned, that would be the end of God and religion. As J. H. Brooke said, 'the God known by science would prove to be the most vulnerable to be overthrown by science'. Once God had been given a role as intervening in the natural world from outside it, the way was open for that role to be narrowed down by scientific investigation to the point where it vanished altogether. Modern atheism arose in part out of the physics of Newton and the metaphysics of Descartes. Unfortunately, in their attempt to use the new science of mechanics as the foundation for religion and the existence of God, they both contributed the seeds for undermining religion in the eighteenth century. The rational religion of Deism proved to be the slippery slope towards atheism, the denial of God.

2.3   DARWIN: SCIENCE AND RELIGION IN TENSION

Charles Darwin and his context

An evolutionary universe is the basic horizon or framework within which we all understand our lives today. Modern science sees the whole cosmos as emerging through the processes of evolutionary change, from the initial Big Bang to complex living things. Biological evolution is the scientific theory that all organisms, all living things, are related by common descent. Evolution means that there is a great multiplicity and diversity of species because organisms change from generation to generation and in different ways. Charles Darwin (1809–1882) was not the first naturalist to think of organic evolution. Jean Baptiste de Lamarck (1744–1829) had already argued that creatures evolved by passing on characteristics they had acquired during their lifetime in adapting to different environments. So a body-builder could pass on the acquired muscles to his/her offspring. Darwin proposed that evolutionary change does not occur through passing on acquired characteristics but through passing on *inherited* characteristics. So our body-builder would not pass on big muscles but might pass on his/her tall stature or short temper. Darwin was the first to give a convincing account of the mechanism, natural selection, by which the great varieties of life forms have come about. He argued that some inherited characteristics gave an edge in the struggle for survival. Darwin called this process by which inherited variations lead to better adaptation 'natural selection'. All species, including the human species, result from a long process of biological evolution.

Darwin's theory of evolution caused a storm of controversy in his own time, polarising people to be passionately for and against, and we are still wrestling with the consequences today. Darwin posed a fundamental question to Christian theology about the origins and the nature of humanity in the latter half of the nineteenth century. Does evolution rule out the existence of

God the Creator? Evolution, more than any other scientific theory, posed a serious challenge to the Christian doctrine of creation, that God is the author of all life, and that human life has a privileged position as the masterpiece of God's creation. It appeared to some to signal the demise of religion, the definitive revelation of a godless world. For many, it reinforced the 'conflict' or 'warfare' model of the interplay between science and religion still present in folklore and legend today. For example, the erroneous belief that Darwin's theory was accepted by scientists and rejected by religious people; some religious thinkers accepted it and some scientists rejected it as flawed science. The reception of Darwin illustrates how science is related to and is affected by the wider cultural context, the social, spiritual and moral considerations of the age. No scientific discoveries take place in a social vacuum, so we must first outline the historical context, the background out of which Darwin's ideas on evolution emerged.

Design in the world of the nineteenth century
As we have seen, the eighteenth century was dominated by the Newtonian model of a regular and ordered mechanical universe that was linked to the rise of Deism. William Paley wrote a famous book on *Natural Theology* (1802), which vigorously defended the design argument; it had a profound influence on popular religious thought in the early part of the nineteenth century and also impressed Darwin. For Paley, Newton's mechanical world suggested the metaphor of a watch: if you found a watch on the heath, you would conclude that the intricate mechanism was constructed for a purpose. Paley argued from the watch, which pointed to a watchmaker, to the world that pointed to a divine Designer. The argument from design was based on the wonderful way in which living things were put together and the way they seemed fitted to their environment, like the way the various parts of a watch fit together. He was impressed by the complexity of the human body, the intricacy of the human organs, like the eye and heart

and the harmony of means to the ends for which they were designed. The intricacies of nature are evidence for God. Paley's argument had a powerful appeal due to the fascination with machinery and their design during the Industrial Revolution. Darwin's theory challenged these theological descriptions of nature and proposed natural selection as an alternative to the design argument, that creatures were individually designed and created by God.

Until the end of the eighteenth century it was generally accepted that nature was fixed and the world was young, less than six thousand years old and created more or less in its present form. 'Fixed species' and 'special creation' summed up their ideas. Plant and animal species were fixed in the form in which God had created them separately from the beginning; no new species could come from another. Humans were God's special creation, set apart from nature and superior to it, made in the image of God. Such ideas were in line with a literal interpretation of the Book of Genesis, that creation was a once-for-all act that established an unchanging order in nature. James Ussher, the Archbishop of Armagh, calculated the age of the earth by adding up the ages of people in the family trees in Genesis. The accepted date for creation, 4004 BC, appeared in the margins of old Bibles. Later developments in geology and biology increasingly challenged these views in the nineteenth century.

It became clear from geological discoveries of fossils and rock strata that the earth was much older than the popular view. What were the implications of geology for the interpretation of Genesis? Great efforts were made to reconcile the growing evidence of a very long history of the earth with the Bible story of creation. 'Concordism' was the name given to the various attempts to harmonise religion with the growing sciences by interpreting biblical texts as if they were scientific data. Belief in the biblical account of creation provided pre-suppositions about divine intervention that coloured scientific inquiry. 'Catastrophists' believed in successive acts of creation, corresponding to the different rock strata, followed by catastrophes, like Noah's flood, which shaped the surface of our earth. William Smith (1769–1839) took the six days of creation in Genesis 1 to mean six geological epochs; geological change took place by the direct intervention of God. Charles Lyell wrote *Principles of Geology* in 1830 and took the opposite view; he was convinced that the earth was a lot older than six thousand years. He argued that the process of geological change was going on all the time over vast periods of time; there is no need for separate acts of creation to account for the different strata and fossils. This interpretation of change as a continuous process over time was called 'uniformitarianism'. Fossil records were also disturbing in that they showed evidence of extinct species; catastrophism could account for that and Darwin accepted this for a while. However, the irregular geographical distribution of species was difficult to square with a special creation. Darwin was persuaded by Lyell's arguments for an ancient earth, that a natural process of gradual change formed the earth's rocks over long periods of time.

It was believed that the one thing the advances in science could not explain was the origin of life and especially human life. The natural process may not need God but the origin of life did; only theology could explain the origin of species. However, Darwin was to propose a related thesis to Lyell's for living things: they too have evolved slowly over long periods of time in the past. 'Concordism' began to unravel with the growing evidence from the sciences that natural forces formed the earth over time and perhaps living things too had a parallel natural history. These controversies concerning Genesis and the geological record formed part of the background to Darwin.

Darwin and evolution

Charles Darwin began his career as a squeamish medical student in Edinburgh, unable to cope with medical procedures like operations and body dissections. He left for Christ's College, Cambridge, intending to study for ministry in the Church of England. In 1831, at the age of twenty-three, he was offered a place on board the HMS Beagle, as a naturalist, to explore wildlife in South America. From 1831–1836 he made an extensive study of nature collecting specimens of rocks, fossils and wildlife, especially from the Galapagos Islands, which he sent back to England. When he left on the voyage he accepted the common view of fixed species and special creation; that God had separately created different species with characteristics suited to their environment. His later reflections on his Galapagos investigations into the peculiarity of the species on the different islands were critical in his development of his theory of evolution. Darwin collected a number of birds that looked like finches, having different characteristics, from different islands. He was startled when told by an expert that the different samples belonged to different *species*. The only plausible explanation was that they derived from one species, blown across from mainland South America, where they developed separately on their different islands. This led him to the conclusion that one species must indeed develop out of another. His task over the next twenty years was to collect the evidence and develop a theory of *how*, the mechanism by which change took place.

Thomas Malthus' *Essay on the Principle of Population* (1798) influenced Darwin's thinking on species at a crucial juncture. Malthus argued that struggle and competition in nature is the key to the survival of a species. Populations increase faster than available resources such as food and space. Competition meant that those species that are best adapted to their environment are more likely to survive. Darwin now had the mechanism he needed, 'natural selection', which could explain the apparent chance variations in characteristics within a species: those variations, which helped survival, would be preserved, those which did not would be gradually wiped out. Those who survive will pass on these characteristics to the next generation. Natural selection could explain the extinction of species in the fossil record and the formation of new ones, without the need for catastrophism or divine intervention. All living species have emerged over a long period of time from a complex process of biological change.

In 1859 Darwin produced his landmark book *The Origin of the Species* in which he set out his theory of the evolution of species by means of natural selection, with a wealth of supporting evidence. Darwin was familiar with 'artificial selection', the breeding of racehorses and domestic animals for special characteristics like speed or endurance. By analogy with artificial selection, Darwin coined the phrase 'natural selection'. He now had a model for the origin of species and he applied his theory to interpreting the fossil record and the geographical distribution of organisms. Darwin sets out his main arguments in the second and third chapters of the *Origin*:

a   Competition: All living species produce too many offspring to survive to maturity and reproduce. There is competition and struggle for scarce resources and to avoid predators. What factors affect survival?

b   Variation: Offspring are not exact copies but differ from their parents, for example, colour, shape of beak or length of legs. Some random variations may give a competitive advantage (taller, quicker, stronger) in the struggle for survival. 'Nature selects', the better adapted survive and reproduce.

c   Heredity: Many of these favourable characteristics are passed on, inherited from one generation to another. The longest living will reproduce the most; so unfavourable characteristics are gradually eliminated. Darwin defined natural selection as 'the preservation of favourable variations and the rejection of injurious variations'.

d   New Species: The process of natural selection can lead over time to new species, through the accumulation of a number of tiny improvements. More and more of the population will possess such characteristics, resulting in a gradual change or 'evolution'. Darwin called this change 'descent with modification'. The variations that lead to different species are completely random suggesting the workings of nature are accidental and irrational. Today the source of these variations is known as genetic mutations that can be attributed to chance.

The result is a 'branching-tree' view of evolution, based on random undirected variations, not a 'special creation' and not a 'ladder of progress', a predictable unfolding of possibilities. Darwin realised that his theory had flaws, such as gaps in the fossil record. There appeared to be no direct evidence for transitional states between species, the kind of gradual process of change that his theory predicted. He had also no idea *how* characteristics are inherited. Knowing nothing of the mechanisms of heredity, he had a theory of blending inheritance; he thought parental characteristics were inherited in the blood, so rare variations could be diluted out; the way red colour mixed with water becomes pink. This contributed to the lack of acceptance of Darwin in the late nineteenth century. Gregor Mendel (1822–1884), a monk from Moravia, published a paper on the inheritance of characteristics in the garden pea. He showed that inherited characteristics were transmitted as units; each higher organism had a pair of units (now called genes) for each inherited characteristic. A particular gene (e.g. brown eyes) may be expressed or lie dormant, but is not diluted out. Changes in genes, called mutations, occurred randomly and were the source of novelty, which allowed for the possibility of evolutionary change.

The challenge of Darwin to Christianity

Though he hardly mentioned humans in the *Origin* the implications for our species became clear in his other major work *Descent of Man* (1871). There were no fixed species or special creation, the human was not set apart from the rest of nature and was not an exception to biological laws. No fundamental biological distinction could be made between humans and animals in terms of their origin and development. Darwin's account of natural selection and the 'survival of the fittest' suggested that creation took place through a series of random and accidental events. Living species were a 'series of successful mistakes'. Where was the guiding hand of God in this process? Darwin's theory placed in doubt the trustworthiness of the Bible and in particular, the long-standing literal interpretation of the creation stories in Genesis. We must now outline the specific difficulties which Darwin's theory of evolution raised for the Christian religion in his time:

a. The challenge to design: Natural selection undermined the notion that God individually designed creatures; there is no externally determined purpose in their survival. It is a blind, impersonal process indifferent to life and humanity. Species flourish or decline depending upon their ability to adapt to their environments. Darwin showed that adaptation could account for apparent design, so undermining Paley's argument. You could no longer argue directly from the ingenuity of the design or the way creatures are adapted to their environment to the Designer God. Development took place through a series of random or accidental events in which it was impossible to see the guiding hand of God. With natural selection, the origin and adaptive nature of living things could be accounted for solely in terms of natural laws and natural processes. The fact that individuals struggle for survival and that most lose out, points to the basic cruelty and wastage of the universe. Where was divine providence? Evolution appeared to be contrary to the good God who created the world for a purpose and whose hand could be discovered within it.

b. The challenge to biblical literalism: Darwin's theory challenged the literal interpretation of Genesis. The hermeneutical question came to the fore once more, as it did in the Galileo debate. The slow process of evolution over millions of years cannot be reconciled with the seven days of creation and a young earth. Lyell showed the earth is very old, so no literal reading of the Bible could accord with the scientific account. As regard living things, Darwin undermined biblical ideas on fixed species and special creation. It could not account for ancient life forms within the fossil record. Creation was not a relatively recent once-for-all act that established a static and unchanging order of nature. Nature is evolving, dynamic and changing: some species, which exist today, did not in the distant past and many species which existed in the past, like the dinosaurs, no longer do so today. An urgent issue, then, in assessing evolution from a Christian perspective centred on the nature and authority of the Bible and how it was to be interpreted.

c. The challenge to human dignity: Darwin challenged the unique status of the human species made in the image of God. Humans were unique because of the immortality of their souls, their superior intelligence and their freedom to make moral choices. Human beings could no longer be seen as set apart, the masterpieces of God's creation, but the product of chance and accidental forces. Not being exempt from the processes of nature, humans are descended from other life forms and are now dominant because of their superior ability to survive. Evolution implied that some higher primates and humans shared a common ancestor, rather than humans coming from a unique act of creation. The value and dignity of the human person as a moral being appeared to be denied by natural selection. Copernican astronomy had demoted humanity from the centre of the universe and now Darwinian evolution had threatened the uniqueness and special status of the human being in nature.

Religious responses to Darwin

It would be wrong to perpetuate the legend that all scientists were for Darwin and all religious people implacably against him, if for no other reason than that many scientists were believers. His book got a great variety of reactions both from scientists and public alike and there were many conflicting interpretations of its implications. There were Christians both for and against; some welcomed it as a further step in tracing how God had created the world. For others it was a bombshell, an atheistic doctrine threatening to those who saw God as the designer of everything. There were some Christian thinkers who immediately celebrated evolution. They were not all committed to 'special creation', that God had designed every single creature exactly in the form they were now known in the present by naturalists. Charles Kingsley said it was as noble of God that he created creatures capable of self-development as to think that God needed to intervene in order to produce new species. Darwin included his comment in the last chapter to the second edition of *Origins*. In the words of Frederick Temple, later to become Archbishop of Canterbury, speaking of the evolution of living creatures 'God made them make themselves'. Many saw the evolutionary model as a healthy corrective to the flawed Deism of the previous century. A fundamental difference between Darwin and the deists was that he could no longer accept the argument from design, since his theory of natural selection took away the need for an external designer. Evolution emphasised the *immanence* of God, the indwelling of God in Creation, weaker in the clockmaker model that in the hands of the deists exaggerated the transcendence of God. Evolution stressed God's continuous activity, not the infrequent winding of a clock. Many influential churchmen of the time in the Church of England saw no necessary conflict between evolution and Christian faith. More liberal Christians accepted evolution as the revelation of God's wonderful way of creating the world. God used the processes of evolution to carry out the divine purpose of creating a world in which there could be creatures like ourselves.

The Catholic Church in the nineteenth century reacted negatively to evolution, seeing it as an example of the materialist and secularist agenda of the age. The Pontifical Biblical

Commission of 1909 insisted on the historical character of the earlier chapters of Genesis giving it a literal interpretation so it teaches scientific truth. The Church gradually assimilated the new methods of Biblical research. Biblical scholarship uncovered the historical and cultural context of the Bible stories; Genesis does not contain history in the modern sense and calls for the investigation of how the ancient peoples of the East thought and expressed their ideas. By 1950 the encyclical *Humani Generis* held that evolution was an 'open question' and that there was no opposition between evolution and creation, but with qualifications. Evolution is an open question as regards the development of the human body from lower forms of life, but it forbids speculations about the human soul. The Church wanted to safeguard the spiritual nature of the human being made in the image of God, 'the only creature that God willed for itself'. A person has value *per se* and cannot be a means to an end or an instrument to be manipulated either by the species or by society. The whole person has dignity because of the soul, which is immediately created by God and is immortal.

The Wilberforce – Huxley debate on evolution

Evolutionary theory raised key questions concerning the nature and authority of the Bible, and of Genesis in particular. Conservative Christians defended the literal truth of the Bible and so rejected all forms of evolution out of hand as part of an atheistic agenda. The polarisation of views on evolution is illustrated by the legendary debate on *Origins* that took place in Oxford on June 30, 1860 between the Bishop of Oxford, Samuel Wilberforce, and Darwin's friend and champion, T. H. Huxley. The story goes that during an acrimonious debate, Wilberforce ridiculed evolution when he asked Huxley whether he was descended from an ape on his grandfather's or grandmother's side? Huxley supposedly replied that he would rather have an ape for a grandfather than a bishop! The exchange between Wilberforce and Huxley was later fabricated into a cultural myth, reinforcing the 'warfare' model of their relationship. Recent historical studies suggest that this was a deliberate caricature designed to show the so-called triumph of atheistic science over a backward Church. The background of the debate concerned the struggle for supremacy in educational matters, between the increasing professionalism in science and the amateur naturalists, many of whom were churchmen. Huxley and his friends promoted a scientific naturalism, the victory of scepticism over religion, since evolution could now be closely associated with unbelief. He was opposed to the privileged position of the Anglican Church in universities like Oxbridge. Known as 'Darwin's bulldog', he resented ecclesiastical intrusion into science and saw clericalism as the enemy of science. The coalition of evolution and the hostility to religion made evolutionary theory appear to be impossible to reconcile with Christian faith. The impact of Darwin was to promote a naturalistic view among many scientists who turned him into a propagandist for a scientific atheism. Ernest Haeckel, in *The Riddle of the Universe* of 1899 popularised Darwin's theory of evolution and celebrated it as the triumph of science over the superstition of religion. He promoted a view now known as 'scientific materialism'. All knowledge and reality are the products of the material world and are absolutely determined by the laws of nature.

Darwin himself believed that God designed the laws of the evolutionary process, but not the detailed structures of each organism, leaving the details to chance. At the end of *Origins* he expressed a sense of wonder at the grandeur of the natural order 'breathed by the Creator' which could be seen as a form of natural religion. Despite the controversies caused by his theory, Darwin was greatly respected by his peers, and his ideas formed the focus for the scientific and intellectual ferment of his day. He died in 1882 and was buried a short distance away from Isaac Newton in Westminster Abbey.

Darwin's ideas, like those of Newton, spread far beyond his science and extravagant claims were made for evolution in terms of morality and social organisation. Evolution became a symbol of the Victorian belief in the inevitability of progress; competition in business reflected the natural outworking of competition in nature. Herbert Spencer used the phrase 'survival of the fittest' to describe the application of natural selection to moral and social questions, known as 'Social Darwinism'. The implication of natural selection, for Spencer, was that human society should follow the struggle for survival in nature, so those not strong enough should be allowed to die. Those who were most fit should not be hindered in their progress by the less able. He opposed the Poor Laws and state education, since they benefited those least fit to take care of themselves. The 'survival of the fittest' was imported from biology into the moral and social order and used to justify ruthless economic competition and colonial aggression. In this he went beyond anything that Darwin advocated in his theory. In opposition to Spencer, many argued that appealing to evolutionary ideas to justify ethical and political systems committed the 'naturalistic fallacy', the deriving an 'ought' from an 'is'. The evidence of evolution pointed to what in fact did happen, but that did not imply it could be used as a basis for what *ought* to happen. Biology tells us that we evolved, but what makes us human and how we are to organise and behave in society is not determined by biology.

Neo-Darwinism in the twenty-first century

The twentieth-century science of Genetics applied to the modified theory of Darwin led to a new synthesis known as Neo-Darwinism. Natural selection and genetic variation are understood today to be the major factors in driving evolutionary change. The insights of molecular biology, especially after the discovery of DNA, have been integrated into the new synthesis. An important issue today concerns the speed of evolutionary change. Darwin's general theory assumed a gradual smooth movement, but there were puzzling gaps in the fossil record. Stephen J. Gould and Niles Eldredge have developed a theory of 'punctuated equilibrium'. Far from always evolving gradually and slowly, species tend to remain stable for long periods; then these stable periods are 'punctuated' by relatively rapid periods of change. For many Neo-Darwinists evolutionary theory is a competitive theory, that is, it is a complete and sufficient account of the origins of life and excludes any other. Theology today has a vigorous dialogue with evolutionary biology. The crucial question is how can we think of God within the evolutionary worldview described by biological science? Neo-Darwinism has become the main challenge to religious belief in a creator God in the twenty first century.

A well-known contemporary exponent of the implications of the new biology for religion is the Oxford zoologist, Richard Dawkins. Dawkins writes movingly and eloquently on the awe-inspiring and creative process that is biological evolution. The most complex, wonderful and intricate creatures have emerged from a long natural process in an amazing way. Dawkins espouses the conflict model of the relationship between religion and science: there is no justification for going beyond the evolutionary process to posit the existence of a designer God. For Dawkins, religion is a scientific theory to explain the universe, existence and life. So the 'hypothesis' of God is a scientific hypothesis in competition with evolutionary theory by natural selection: 'God and natural selection are the only workable theories we have of why we exist'. In *The Blind Watchmaker* he dismisses the design argument, that order and design in nature point to a divine 'watchmaker', first put forward by William Paley. More and more complex organisms can be formed by the application of a few simple principles, chance variations and natural selection. The God hypothesis, the divine designer, is rejected as inferior to evolution; we do not need to call on God if chance and blind natural selection can account for all the diverse species of life, including ourselves. Religious explanations were once credible, but not any longer and they should now be abandoned as outdated and irrational.

Evolution has eliminated any remaining intellectual respectability from the idea of God.

In another best-selling book, *The Selfish Gene,* he explores further the genetic base of evolution. Our genes are inherently selfish, not in a morally pejorative sense, but in the sense that their task is to promote survival and successful reproduction. The human bodies through which genes operate can then be thought of as their 'survival suits'. In a recent book, *The Devil's Chaplain,* Dawkins refers to Darwin's own misgivings that evolutionary theory eliminated design and may have atheistic implications. However, Darwin claimed that, though natural selection may account for the details of design, he favoured the idea that the laws of nature were designed.

Dawkins' claim that religion is a scientific theory, as a competing 'explanation for facts about the universe and life' is very questionable. Dawkins has collapsed the distinction between two different kinds of explanation, treating them as alternatives. This is to commit a *type error* in explanation. Dawkins takes a mechanism (chance and natural selection) accounting for adaptation as a reason for dismissing any idea of design. But there is no logical conflict between explanations of *mechanisms* and explanations of the plans or purposes of an *agent.* Creation is the act of an agent, God causing things to exist; evolution is the mechanism, the process by which living things came to be. Biology is not omnicompetent to answer all our questions concerning the meaning and purpose of life because reality is multi-layered and there are other descriptions of the real.

Dawkins espouses a form of 'evolutionism', that is, he professes a materialist philosophy and seeks to ground it in the theory of evolution. The claim is that evolutionary theory is inseparable from a scientific materialist philosophy. 'Evolutionism' is an alternative secular religion. This is a confusion or a 'conflation' of science with a materialist or secularist religion. Evolution, as a scientific theory, neither supports nor contradicts belief in a designer God. Design or purpose is not part of the scientific description of evolution, but that does not exclude it from other levels of explanation.

Dawkins is reductionist in arguing that the material world is all there is and the spiritual dimension is denied. We are 'nothing but' the genetic material that make us up. This is also a metaphysical claim which science cannot substantiate as it is only concerned with material processes. The claim that the whole, higher functions like mind and consciousness, can be fully explained by appeal to the parts, our genes is a reductionist argument. Though our genes may be geared toward survival, the mind may value the good, the true and the beautiful irrespective of their survival value. Humans participate in life at a different level, the level of culture, which cannot be reduced to the lowest common denominator

The Neo-Darwinist claim that evolution is blind and directionless rules out design and purpose, and hence rules out God. A difficulty for its exponents is to explain the rise of complexity. Evolution shows a puzzling progression toward greater complexity rather than less, under the random forces of genetic mutations and natural selection. Neo-Darwinists like Gould and Dawkins deny that the rise in complexity is 'progress' and this can be accounted for by blind natural processes. Gould's materialism compels him to see human consciousness as 'but a tiny, late-arising twig' on the bush of evolving life. Evolutionary theists argue that faith and evolution are compatible. They see the providential hand of God in the mysterious processes of evolution, moving the creation from inert matter, to life and consciousness. Matter has produced us and yet we have the capacity to understand the process and direct it. The particulars of our evolutionary past have influenced how we have arrived and what we have inherited; but they are not central for defining who we are or what our relationship to God is like. With the arrival of our species, with all the new possibilities for freedom, moral perception, aesthetic appreciation and our capacity for love, it is clear that evolution emerged onto a new plane.

2.4 ECOLOGY: SCIENCE AND RELIGION IN DIALOGUE

The ecological crisis

The religious doctrine of Creation (in Judaism, Christianity and Islam) supplies the theological context for many contemporary questions concerning the interplay of religion and science today, especially questions in evolution, cosmology, bioethics and ecology. The question of ecology, the relationship between human beings and the earth, has become a troubling one disclosing a crisis of life on our planet. Ecology comes from the Greek root *oikos* meaning 'home', our planet. It refers to the study of the complex conditions necessary for the surviving and thriving of living things. Ecology highlights the interconnectedness of everything in the one web of planetary life. It is the study of our planet as a 'community of communities'.

The view of planet earth from space has awakened our consciousness to the beauty and at the same time, the fragility and vulnerability of the earth our home. It is like a tiny, precious garden in the immensity of space, but a garden threatened by nuclear destruction, the greenhouse effect and the breakdown of the ozone layer. The ecological crisis on our planet earth presents a new urgency to contemporary discussions on science and religion. There is a growing concern about the uses to which science and technology are being put and their negative effects on our environment. The main threats to our natural environment are the following: the pollution of land, water and air, the destruction of the rain forests, the erosion of the soil, the loss of sources of fresh water, the spread of deserts, the alarming rate of species extinction, global warming, and the thinning of the ozone layer. Added to that, the growing human population contributes to and exacerbates the environmental threats. Humans escape the laws that govern the biosphere-in-balance in the sense that nature has no defence against the disruptive potential of human beings. Humans also have the technical capacity to invent weapons of mass destruction, whether nuclear, biological or chemical, with terrifying implications for the biosphere.

In the light of this stark analysis, there is a pressing need for human beings to arrive at a shared concern for the natural world and to address the problem that the life systems on our planet are in grave danger of irreversible collapse. The ecological crisis describes the breakdown in a series of relationships: between the person in the human community, the human community in the earth community, and the earth community in the cosmos. Ecology and the ethical questions it raises form a very fruitful area of dialogue where science and theology make common cause today.

The origins of the ecological crisis: from wonderland to wasteland.
Who is responsible for the ecological crisis? There are conflicting claims: a. science and technology are to blame; b. religion also has contributed to the crisis.

a.   The enchantment of technology
Science is often blamed for the crisis because it has produced the industrial-technological complex responsible for much environmental abuse. Ever since the industrial revolution, science and technology have increasingly manipulated and exploited the natural world in the name of economic progress. People sometimes draw a distinction between pure science, as the pursuit of truth for its own sake, and technology as the application of science to practical problems. Technology implies two things: power and progress. It means increasing power over the environment, which results in an advance or progress of some kind, a more efficient way of doing things; the tractor is an improvement on the plough horse. There is an ambivalence about the value of technology in Western society today. On the one hand we are the beneficiaries of impressive technological contributions in medicine, healthcare, food production,

electronics, communications and so on. Technology is benign and has transformed our world for the better. On the other hand, public concern focuses on the damage done to our global environment by modern technology. Furthermore, there is the public anxiety raised by advances in genetics and human reproduction. Hence the pessimistic view of the 'deification of technology': that technology is out of control and, if left unchecked, could ultimately result in the destruction of the human and the earth community. These two views bring to light that questions of value are embedded in technology. Modern technology is shaped by the values of our culture. There is a socio-political dimension to the ecological crisis in the sense that it is from the ways humans have organised their lives in Western society that the crisis in nature arises. The economic imperative in industrial nations to increase their yearly GNP has placed enormous pressures on dwindling, non-renewable natural resources. The drive towards progress and limitless development is draining the earth's resources at an alarming rate. This is especially evident in the exploitation of the Third World for cheap raw materials to feed the consumerism of the wealthy nations. To a great extent, the creed of unlimited economic progress drives the industrial, agricultural and military habits that are ruining the biosphere. It is too naïve to blame science as such for the ecological crisis. After all, it is scientific analysis in the first place that has alerted us to the extent and the depth of the crisis. But science, no more than technology, is not value free: scientific research is not the detached pursuit of pure knowledge. Science is linked with politics and with the imperatives of the market place, and scientists belong within the political context. Science makes value judgements in prioritising areas of research, in the sources of funding and the methods they use in carrying it out.

The rise of technology has allowed us to fundamentally change the natural world and control it like a machine with no intrinsic value. The reasons for this can be traced back to the physics of the seventeenth century, to the Cartesian split between subject and object, which divided the human from the natural world. The classical mechanical view of the lifeless material world, composed of mass and extension, means that nature is rigidly determined and so is meaningless. Humans are spiritual and so are value-creating and meaning-projecting beings. The cosmos has no intrinsic meaning or value and is little more than the stage in which the human drama takes place. The value it has is purely instrumental, something useful for our purposes to fulfil human desires, and so it becomes vulnerable to human abuse. The absolute split is illustrated by Descartes' belief that animals were machines. This anthropocentric view, which places an exaggerated emphasis on ourselves, robs the non-human world of its intrinsic worth.

The dualistic split is also furthered by the distinction of primary and secondary qualities. Primary qualities are objective in nature and can be measured: mass, momentum, shape and position. This is unlike secondary qualities that are dependent on the perceiving human subject: colour, taste, sound, smell and texture. There is an unbridgeable gap between the perceiving and valuing subject 'in here' and the real, material and valueless world 'out there'. The human is an alien, a stranger in the cosmos, an exception to the deterministic laws, who gives the world no other value than that of being important for human projects. Human values, aesthetic sensibility, moods and feelings are not really real and so provide no basis for an ecological ethic. The divorce of the human mind from nature, that the human is an alien in the cosmos, needs to be challenged if we are to construct an ecological ethic. Ecological concern demands that unless we treat the earth as our home we will have little incentive to care for it, and a religious vision can help us. To do this we need a story of the cosmos that recognises we live in a value-permeated universe that is home to us and to all life forms.

b. Deism and an inadequate theology of creation

Religion is also blamed for the ecological crisis, even if not directly, at least through its neglect and indifference to the natural world. The churches, synagogues and mosques have traditionally paid little attention to ecological issues. Their religious texts appear to have little to say about environmental destruction and in promoting the care of the earth. It has been argued that the otherworldly focus of the major religions has led to the neglect of the natural world; emphasis on the supernatural has made us ignore this world for the sake of the next. Some religious people think that environmental concern is purely of secular interest, a distraction from human issues of justice and peace. In the case of Christianity this neglects appears anomalous. In its accent on creation, the incarnation of the Word, the resurrection of the body, and sacramental presence, Christian faith is earthy in its engagement with the material universe.

Indeed some have gone further in suggesting that religion, far from being part of the solution, is part of the cause of the ecological crisis. Some have criticised the doctrine of creation as having a very negative influence on attitudes towards nature. Critics say that the doctrine has contributed to the exploitation of the environment to further scientific and technological advances. An historian Lynn White in the 1960s wrote an influential essay on the emerging ecological crisis. He argued that the exploitative outlook originates in the Judeo-Christian tradition's teaching from the Bible. Genesis 1:26-27 appears to give the right to human beings to exercise dominion over and subdue the earth. As a consequence, the Western world has determined that nature exists in order to serve humans. Christianity's anthropocentric view of creation contributes to a split of humans from nature. By stressing the dominion of humanity over nature, Christianity has sanctioned an ethic of exploitation and has fostered science and technology as instruments of that exploitation. For White, Christianity bears a huge burden of guilt for the ecological crisis. His essay had a very negative effect on the shaping of popular scientific attitudes towards Christianity in particular.

The argument is now seen as seriously flawed. A closer reading of the Genesis text encourages us to practice 'stewardship', to take care of nature in the name of the Creator. 'Dominion' does not mean domination; rather it means that humans are the stewards of creation in partnership with God. Humans are made in the 'image of God', which means that our proper role is to be God's representatives to the natural world. We have a delegated authority from God as his stewards or managers of the created world. Since God is the sustainer of life, the Bible demands that we his stewards imitate God in sustaining the earth. There is then no justification in the Bible for dominating and abusing the earth. The thrust of many Biblical passages is to remind us of our duty to respect and nurture the natural world. The doctrine of creation affirms the importance of human responsibility towards the environment; creation is entrusted to human beings for safekeeping and tending. A key way of understanding the role of human beings in creation is to see them as 'co-creators' with God in the processes of nature. God does not rule creation by divine dictate, but he is a covenant-making God who rules by collaboration and by participation. Science can provide the means by which humans can co-operate and act as co-creators with God; it implies the intelligent use of scientific knowledge to forego selfish and exploitative ends and to achieve ecological wholeness. Nature is not of our making and so can never be just a means to a selfish human end, because it has intrinsic value as the gift of an intelligent Creator. The Judeo-Christian tradition is not responsible for humanity's domination of nature. Far from being an enemy of ecology, Christian theology encourages an ethic of stewardship opposed to an ethic of domination.

We have seen the unfortunate consequences of the Cartesian split between the human and natural world that encouraged an exploitative agenda in science and technology. There is also a religious dualism of God and nature in the form of a Deist view of creation, which has contributed to the ecological crisis. As we have outlined (2.2), Newton's emphasis on a clockwork universe was closely linked to the rise of Deism. God designed and created the world in the beginning, but he is located 'outside' the world, which now runs according to the initial laws and no longer requires God's presence or intervention. God no longer acts within the world, as it is autonomous and self-sufficient. Nature no longer speaks of God, 'a natureless view of God and a Godless view of nature'. From a religious viewpoint this is a sombre conclusion and can only be remedied by a proper understanding of creation.

The Christian understanding of creation

The fundamental idea of God that is central to the Jewish, Christian and Muslim traditions is that God is the one and only Creator of everything other than God. The doctrine of creation expresses the belief that the one God is the origin, ground and goal of the universe and everything in it. It is a foundational theme of the Biblical writings, that the God who saves his people in salvation history is also the God who creates all things in the first place. The Hebrew Scriptures tell us that 'in the beginning God created the heavens and the earth' (Gen 1:1). Creation interprets the universe as a gift freely brought into existence by a powerful, loving and personal Creator. The key idea of creation is that of 'bringing into being' that which was not; the universe is not self-originating but the act of a good God. The Bible makes a clear distinction between God as Creator and the world as the creation. In the early Church the doctrine of creation was spelt out in two models: *creatio ex nihilo* (creation out of nothing) and *creatio continua* (continuing creation).

Creation out of nothing

Prominent in the Christian doctrine of creation is the declaration that God created the world *ex nihilo,* out of nothing, rather than out of any pre-existing material. *Creatio ex nihilo* was developed in the second century as a Christian response to Greek cosmology, which did not have the notion of creation. Greek philosophy took it for granted that the universe is eternal and uncreated. God was not a creator for the Greeks, but rather a world architect who ordered and shaped pre-existent material, like an artist with ready raw materials. The word 'cosmos' means order. *Ex nihilo* was opposed to two notions: Plato's idea that matter was co-eternal with God, and to the dualism of the Gnostics, a religious group who saw the world as evil. For the Greeks, there are two equal eternal principles – matter as well as the divine. For Christians, matter is not eternal; God created matter out of nothing, that is, not out of anything pre-existing. The world is not co-eternal with God, because it had a temporal beginning and is distinct from God. God brings into existence that which did not exist before. The doctrine safeguards the transcendence of God and his free agency in willing the existence of something other than himself.

The Neo-Platonists maintained that the world proceeds or 'emanates' from God of necessity, from the necessary overflowing of God's being; it could not be otherwise. For Christians, God could have decided not to create anything; it need not be at all. God freely creates through his choice of this particular world rather than another; it need not be the way it is. This implies the rejection of pantheism, the notion that God and matter are identical. Against the pantheists, Christians held that the world is not divine. It is a creation, brought into existence by God, but is other than God as a distinct reality. The universe is contingent in that it is absolutely dependent on the transcendent God as the sole source of its existence. The world depends on God for its existence, but God does not depend on the world and is independent of his creation. *Creatio ex nihilo* means that God transcends the world and is distinct from the creation; the world is not God, so that there is an enormous gap in being between creatures and the Creator.

The other major concern of the Early Church was Gnostic dualism. It was important to distinguish orthodox Christianity from the Gnostic view that matter was evil – it could not be evil if created by God since all that God creates is good. For the Gnostics the material world is dark, chaotic and evil, and the spiritual, invisible world is all light and good. The Gnostics believed in a supreme good God, who created the spiritual and invisible world, and in a lesser God, who created the visible, material world. The result is a radical dualism between God and the material world, which is inherently evil. God's salvation then for the Gnostics is *from* the evil material universe, which encourages a flight from the world of matter. The Nicene Creed of the fourth century begins with the affirmation of the oneness of God, maker of heaven and earth. The creed maintains, against the dualism of the Gnostics, that the one and only God made all of reality, spiritual as well as material. God redeemed the world by taking on a material human existence in the incarnation of his Son; the incarnation safeguards the goodness of material creation. *Ex nihilo* sees the existence of the world as dependent on a transcendent God who created it, as a free action of his will.

In summary, God created the world out of nothing and not from any pre-existing material. *Ex nihilo* maintained the goodness of the created world against the Gnostic view of matter as evil. Against pantheism, it asserted that the world is not divine or part of God, but is distinct from God. Against the Greek idea that the world is an emanation of God, made from the substance of God, it affirmed that God is transcendent and essentially different from the world.

Continuous creation

Christian theology highlights another key idea in its understanding of creation: God acts continuously to create and sustain the world now and in the future. Creation is not a singular event in the distant past, which is now finished, but it is also a *creatio continua* in that God continues to sustain it in existence. God is continually at work in the universe, which is dependent on him for every moment of its existence. If God ceased to conserve or sustain all creation, it would fall back into nothingness, the creation would cease to exist. It is not as though God was someone who builds a house and then goes away leaving the house to stand on its own. The contingency of the universe, the fact that it need not be, requires the continuous action of God to sustain it in being. The emphasis is not on origins, how things were in the beginning, but on how they are *now* in relation to God. The God-world relationship is a continuing covenant, a real relationship between God and the earth.

Creatio continua stresses the immanence of God, his presence and close relation to the world that he is continuously creating. The idea counteracts the Deist view of creation, that God's only creative act was at the beginning of a static, fixed and deterministic world. The Deist God was external to and separate from creation as he was located 'outside' the world, which he created in the beginning and then left to run on its own. By contrast, *continua* means reality is dynamic and incomplete and the world is in a process of becoming and the future is open to God. The world is filled with novelty, and human choice counts in shaping the future as God acts in nature and history. In the future, God's faithfulness to his creation will bring all of reality to its fulfilment.

In summary, *ex nihilo* emphasises God's transcendence to the world, while *continua* highlights the presence and immanence of God at the heart of the natural world. Creation is not just about the origin of the universe, but the ongoing interaction of God with the world and its dependence upon him.

Religious resources for an ecological ethic

The task of theology in the midst of the crisis is to show that the Christian understanding of creation can provide the religious resources for an ethic sensitive to ecology. Nature is neither divine nor demonic; it is a contingent and not necessarily existent world. God is the immanent Creator, acting in and through the creative processes of the natural world revealed by the sciences. Knowledge of that world through science is itself contingent and never absolute. The full Christian doctrine of creation teaches that God is both immanent in and yet transcends the world. In this unified vision the Creator transcends the world and is not to be identified with it (*ex nihilo*). But the Creator is not remote from the world either (Deism); creation is in close relation with God yet free to be itself (*continua*). There is a paradox in the sense that God exists in everything and is never really distant from his creatures, yet since creatures are unlike God, they are necessarily distant from God. He is the One in 'whom we live and move and have our being' (Acts 17:28). Creation is distinct from, though not separate from, the creator. Theology sees the entire creation, with all its immense diversity and richness, as part of a unified whole; all creatures form one community grounded in their Creator.

What resources can the Christian understanding of creation provide for an ecological ethic? Three points summarise a holistic view of creation:

a. Interconnection: The One God creates the whole cosmos as one diverse but inter-related system. A key principle in ecology asserts that the entire earth community and the human community are bound together in a single destiny. Only in a viable natural world can there be a viable human world; human survival depends on a right relationship with the natural world. Creation is one world, one community of interdependent relationships and so each species has its own unique place. Only if we cherish our connectedness to the wider life-community, and fully appreciate our interdependency with the rest of nature, will we be animated to respect it.

b. Immanence of God in creation: The Creator is present to every part of the cosmos sustaining it in being. Whatever is happening in the world is part of God's activity – there is no separate material world with which he is not concerned. God in-dwells the creation through the power of the Holy Spirit so that the pillage of nature becomes an assault on God. The immanence of God in creation helps to correct the dualism of God and nature that has characterised the Western Christian tradition since Descartes and Newton.

A key principle of the monotheistic religions is that the divine mystery is disclosed not only in sacred texts, but also in the beauty and diversity of nature. A sacramental vision sees nature, at least in rudimentary way, as transparent to God. The richness of religion's symbolic reference to ultimate reality depends on our upholding 'the integrity of creation'. Sacramental symbols taken from nature, like water, earth, air, and light, must retain their wholeness if they are to be transparent to mystery. Therefore, nature's sacramental character gives us an intrinsically religious reason for ecological concern, for maintaining the beauty and diversity of nature. Religions cannot say much about God apart from the riches and variety already present in nature. Thomas Berry argues how impoverished our religions would be if we lived on a lunar landscape. If we lose the natural world, we blunt our sense of God, and we lose the God who transcends us. The book of nature has been closed to us: 'Becoming literate with printed books, we become illiterate in the great book of the universe'. Nature is worth saving because it has intrinsic worth, because it is sacramental, capable of mediating to us the hidden mystery of the divine. Seeing nature as sacramental prevents it from becoming mere stuff of human consumption and exploitation.

c. Humans: stewards and partners with God in creation: The doctrine of creation unambiguously affirms the importance of human responsibility toward the environment. Nature is entrusted to us as gift and we have responsibility for its safe keeping and tending (Gen 2:15). We are earth-keepers, co-creators with God in the work of sustaining the natural world. The human community belongs to the earth community. Science and technology are therefore human means towards worthwhile ends in nature and not ends in themselves. Both are in the service of the human and earth community. Technology offers human beings the ability to impose mastery and control over nature, redirecting it for our own ends.

A goal of ecology then is the sensible use of science and technology to replenish renewable resources for the benefits of humans and of all life forms on our planet. The abundance and fertility of nature is to be enjoyed and not destroyed. Creation must be allowed to re-create, to allow it to recover from overuse by humans. Humans are part of a world of beings, which are all related to one another and reflect something of the mystery of their Creator. The uncritical view, that everything revolves around human beings and is permanently at their disposal, is no longer tenable. Every since Galileo humans are not at the centre of the universe but this anthropocentrism still persists with devastating effects for ecology.

But the opposite view, promoted by a scientific materialism based on evolution, is also untenable. This suggests that humans are simply one species among many others, and they have no more dignity or rights than any other creatures. A human person has no more value or worth than a worm or a fungus; we happen to be at the top of the evolutionary tree for now. The Bible teaches that humans made in the 'image and likeness of God' do have a privileged, but not a domineering place in God's plan or creation. Eco-justice is then inseparable from social justice. The poor and oppressed often suffer due to the technological progress and consumerism of the wealthy nations who exploit indigenous natural resources preventing human liberation. Ecology must also address the additional pressures on the earth's ecosystems from an increasing global population.

Science and theology as ecological partners

If human beings are to survive and thrive, science and theology must recognise they are companions in the ecological crisis and they must work together to resolve it. Theology can play its part by insisting that nature is gift, God's creation and not a human plaything. It is generally acknowledged that a culture of scientific materialism has failed to provide an ecological ethic today. Scientific culture has encouraged our estrangement from the natural world and to a sense of cosmic exile. A scientific materialism provides the intellectual background to many presentations of science today. This is a reductionist view that all biology is reducible to physics and chemistry; all life and mind are the products of accident and humans are nothing but biological machines (see 4.1). The mechanical world-view has resulted in the disenchantment of nature that has contributed to unrestrained technological mastery of the environment. A cosmos of blind physical processes has no spiritual or ethical value; scientific materialism separates beauty from the material world as beauty and all other values are human projections. If the universe is meaningless and purposeless, it is difficult to explain why life can be held to be intrinsically, and not just instrumentally, valuable.

But there are hopeful signs that science and theology can co-operate for the good of the earth. A conference of scientists and theologians held in Washington D.C. in 1992 worked out a common position in their 'Joint Appeal by Science and Religion on the Environment' which they issued in a consensus statement:

> We are people of faith and of science who, for centuries, often have travelled different roads. In a time of environmental crisis, we find these roads converging. As this meeting symbolises, our two ancient, sometimes antagonistic, traditions now reach out to one another in a common endeavour to preserve the home we share.

There is the conviction that the well being of the earth is now in such jeopardy that scientists and theologians alike must work together to put things right. People of faith and science can now see eye to eye on the urgency of this issue and can help in the search for 'wisdom' about our world. 'Wisdom' means grasping the wholeness of things and our place within it in order to articulate an ecological ethics. By itself, science cannot teach us why exactly our natural world should be treasured and preserved, as it is not clear if nature possesses intrinsic value or purpose. While science can give us amazing facts about living things, it cannot give any ethical basis for valuing organisms. Religion can provide us with the moral inspiration to act in an ethical way to care for the earth community. Religious beliefs about right and wrong can provide us with moral 'oughts': because something can be done in science and technology does not mean it ought to be done. The challenge is towards a 'cosmic praxis'. This refers to the human responsibility to shape the world in which we live respecting the integrity of creation, to undo the damage already done and to preserve its biodiversity into the future. A striking plea for ecological wisdom comes from a Cree-Indian Prophecy: 'When the last tree has been cut down; when the last river has been polluted – only then will we realise that money cannot be eaten'.

Islam and creation
Islam is a religion of oneness: the central message is God's unity. The One God, whose sacred name is Allah in Arabic, is the Creator of the universe. The story of creation in the Qur'an is very similar to Genesis in that the world is created in six days. Islam, like Christianity, believes that God brought the whole world into being out of nothing. Creation has its origins in the absolute goodness of Allah, the 'Beneficent', who freely creates this particular world with its unique features and laws. Everything in creation is obedient to the will of God and he

controls the universe through his eternal commands. The whole creation is meaningful and fits together because God created it exactly as he wants it to be; creation is sacred and praises the Creator by being itself in its beauty and diversity.

There is one marked difference with the Judaeo-Christian tradition. In the biblical tradition God is not responsible for evil. God allows it to happen as the free action of his rebellious creatures who turn against him. When Islam says God creates everything, this includes evil as well as good. God punishes those who commit evil even though he is responsible for its existence. God's will is sovereign and so if God wills a human to do evil, it cannot be avoided. Yet, the creature has the duty to struggle against evil. Islam has no doctrine of original sin. There is an inevitable tension between the predetermination of everything by God's will and free will.

The doctrine of the oneness of God is the central organising principle that permeates religious thought and practice. *Tawhid* (Oneness) meaning 'being one' or 'making one' is central to the Islamic understanding of the universe. The Unity of the universe has its origin from God and will return to God. God's commands that govern the world go out from him, achieve their purpose, and return to him. This principle of unity-in-multiplicity resonates with much modern science in organisms, in natural systems and in the rational unity of the cosmos. It is a refusal to see any object, process, or law as existing apart from God, the One. The aim of Islamic science is to show the unity and interrelatedness of everything so that reflecting on the unity of the cosmos people will be led to the Divine Principle of Unity. Both the Qur'an and the natural world speak to us of the power of the Almighty and the Divine Unity.

Nature reveals 'signs' of the Creator, and we can glimpse something of the wisdom of God who has wonderfully designed and ordered the universe. To enable us to understand his creation God has given us guidance: most importantly, revelation through the Qur'an, the literal, spoken words of God to the Prophet Muhammad, which is the absolute truth for Muslims. Then there is God's gift of human intelligence that explains the development of knowledge, of science and technology in Islam. Science studies the acts of the Creator, but it must always be guided by the Qur'an. The purpose of science is to shed light on the works of the Creator and thereby to respect and worship him.

This reveals a major difference between science in the West and in Islam. Western science is secular and autonomous: science gains knowledge through independent inquiry and its results are relative and provisional. Muslim scientists explain the nature of things in terms of their supernatural origin: science is not an end in itself but a means of understanding God and of helping solve the problems of the community. It is subordinate to the absolute infallible truth of the Qur'an as the ultimate court of appeal; the verses contain eternal truths independent of time and contextual setting. Thus, if there is a contradiction between science and the Qur'an then the science is mostly likely to be wrong. Science in Islam does not have the autonomy as the ultimate arbiter of scientific truth as it does in the West. Hence, Darwin's theory of evolution is a great obstacle to Islam because it appears to exclude God and has no basis in the Qur'an. The Qur'an speaks of the special creation of the human by God, a new and unique species who did not evolve from other pre-existing species. Muslims reject evolution because it assumes a continuity between species, between humans and the higher apes, whereas special creation asserts discontinuity and the pre-eminent position of humans created directly by God.

The relationship between Islam and science is a source of tension for Muslim scholars and there is no consensus today. Muslim scientists generally explain created things in terms of their supernatural origin. The tension then exists because modern Western science never refers to God as the Creator, has no God-based moral value-system and teaches evolution. Some Muslims say that modern science is animated by a Western-style materialism; it has no moral values and can only be harmful and dangerous to religious belief. For them, modern science is a godless, secular pursuit that fails to appreciate the limitations of knowledge. A few Muslim scientists have mistakenly tried to find evidence in the Qur'an of ideas belonging to contemporary Western science. This is unwise because Western theories are provisional and subject to change, whereas the Qur'an contains the eternal words of Allah.

But today the majority claims that in principle there is no incompatibility between science and Islam. Once we acknowledge God's ownership over all knowledge, the Work of God (science) and the Word of God (Qur'an) can never be antagonistic to one another. The question for Muslims is how can they best relate to a world dominated by modern science without transgressing the principles of Islam. The religion of Islam seeks to promote the material as well as the spiritual well-being of human beings. Technology is justified as it brings benefits and relief from toil for the community, but it can also be harmful to the environment. The right way for humans to relate to God's creation is contained in the notion of *khalifah*. The human is the *khalifah*, the 'vice-regent' of Allah who holds the earth in trust, to care for it and manage it in the name of the Creator. The Qur'an repeatedly speaks of the need to keep the balance of nature and not upset it. The ecological crisis is the result of wasteful use of precious resources such as water, plants and land. The duty of *khalifah* devolves on governments and organisations as well as individuals. God gives guidance to enable people to distinguish harmful and forbidden acts, because they are destructive and an offence to Allah, from those that are *halal* or approved. It is a huge responsibility and humans must give an account of their stewardship of the resources on the planet.

Select bibliography

Brooke, J. H. *Science and Religion: Some Historical Perspectives*, Cambridge University Press, 1991

Khalid, F. (ed.) *Islam and Ecology*, London: Cassell, 1992

Lindberg, D. and Numbers R. (eds) *God and Nature: Historical Essays on the Encounter between Christianity and Science*, Berkley: University of California Press, 1986

McGrath, A. *Science and Religion: an Introduction*, Oxford: Blackwell, 1999

Poole, M. *Beliefs and Values in Science Education*, Buckingham: OUP, 1995

Richardson, W. M. and Wildman, W. J. (eds) *Religion and Science: History, Method, Dialogue*, London: Routledge, 1996

3

Current Issues for Religion and Science: Origins

3.1   THE DEBATE ABOUT ORIGINS

Why bother about origins?

It is very human for people to wonder about their existence and their place in the cosmos. Men and women of all cultures have tried to understand their lives within a cosmic order in order to make sense of life. There is the felt need to ward off the insecurity caused by the threats of chaos, violence and death. Theories about the origin of the universe (whether ancient or modern) attempt to answer the question of our identity, by describing how the human enterprise fits into the overall scheme of things. Our present identity depends on a foundational narrative or story to relate who we are, where we have come from, and whether we have any lasting significance. Human interest in origins is driven by the need to understand who we are in terms of a vision that binds society together, in terms of a larger meaning and purpose.

Cosmology, though it is a scientific theory about the origins of the cosmos, inevitably raises questions about the meaning and value of human life and so it is at the heart of issues concerning science and religion today. Religious stories of creation in the Bible give us a sacred cosmology that portrays basic relationships between God, human life and the world of nature; it places humankind within a world of meaning, giving our species a sense of purpose. The search for origins contains two questions common to science and religion:

- Beginnings – an account of the past, the origins of universe given by cosmology and the religious doctrine of creation.
- Meaning – the question of purpose and destiny, a meaningful or meaningless universe, the ending of the world and future destiny

In a pluralistic and fragmented world it is clear that we lack a shared story today, an inclusive narrative, a shared sense of identity. Yet, a new comprehensive story is being told, the scientific story of our origins and our common belonging. This story obviously impacts on our theological narratives. We must be careful to distinguish in our discussion scientific theories about the origins of the universe and the religious significance we give to the process.

An overview of current debate on origins

The great advances made by science in the last century have led to a radically new understanding of the cosmos. Above all, there was a dramatic change in our understanding of the age and the dimensions of the universe. Astronomers from Ptolemy, Copernicus, and Galileo and through the eighteenth century assumed that the universe is very small in size and young in age. In the nineteenth century claims from the biblical literalists that the universe was only a few thousand years old conflicted with the evidence from geology, evolutionary theory and fossil records. The Great Telescope at Birr Castle, County Offaly, was built by the Earl of Rosse in the 1840s, and was the largest telescope the in world for seventy years. The telescope provided evidence that distant stellar objects outside the Milky Way were in fact other galaxies, some of which were very large and spiral in shape. In the twentieth century evidence of the immense size and age of the universe has accumulated from cosmology, and new cosmological theories have raised significant issues in relation to religious beliefs. Two of the most important issues to emerge from modern cosmology relate to the Expanding Universe and the 'Anthropic Principle'. We shall deal with these in turn.

Cosmology
The science of cosmology is the physics of the origin and structure of the universe as a whole. Cosmology asks three basic questions:

1   How did the universe begin? Big Bang Theory
2   How did it get to its present state? Expanding and cooling universe
3   What is its future? Big Crunch or Heat Death

An expanding universe
The discovery that the universe is expanding is one of the great scientific revolutions of the twentieth century. We are learning to see the world in an entirely different way from our ancestors, a view that demands a shift in our mindset. The older view saw the universe as static and fixed, unchanging and stable and some people thought it was eternal, that it had no beginning. Newton saw the universe as contained in a fixed frame by God. Modern cosmology has laid to rest the idea of an eternally existing universe; the universe has not existed forever but did have a definite beginning in the very distant past. Part of the radical new picture is the sheer scale of the universe and its astonishing origins fifteen billion years ago.

The theoretical model to explain an expanding universe is the standard 'Big Bang' Theory or the 'Flaring Forth'; it raises profound questions about the origin and destiny of the universe. The fact that the universe is expanding suggested to scientists that the expansion started out from an extremely compressed and dense state of matter. Cosmology tells us that the universe began with a cosmic explosion called the Big Bang, that everything was concentrated in a dense point and out of this explosion came everything: space, time, matter and energy. Since then the universe has been expanding rapidly and cooling. We live in an ever-expanding universe, with galaxies accelerating away from us and from each other at enormous speeds. It exploded like an expanding balloon of space-time and as it began to cool, the basic forces of gravity, electricity and magnetism and the strong and weak nuclear forces were created. An illustration might be to paint spots on a balloon and blow it up. As the balloon expands, the spots recede from each other and the more distantly related spots recede more rapidly. The universe is estimated to consist of ten billion galaxies, each composed of billions of stars and gas clouds where stars are formed. Yet, all this matter is but an exception to the rule of emptiness, grains of sand spread thinly through a void. Our own galaxy, the Milky Way, is spiral in shape and rotates; it is thought to contain one hundred billion stars, and to be about one hundred thousand light years in diameter.

Our Sun is a smallish star, situated about thirty-two thousand light years from the centre of the galaxy, near the edge of one of the spiral arms. We are in a much larger and longer-lived universe than we could ever imagine. A remarkable feature of the universe is that to look out into space is to look back in time. If I observe a galaxy ten million light years away, I observe it as it was ten million years ago, when the light started its journey towards me, and not as it is now. Light from the sun takes nine minutes to arrive on our planet, so we see the sun as it was nine minutes ago. If we could run the universe backwards in time, like showing a film backwards, what would we see? The observation that the universe is expanding leads to the proposition that, going backwards in time, there was a moment in the distant past (about fifteen billion years ago) when the whole universe was concentrated into a single point. As we move back in physical time 't', the temperature and density of the universe would soar as the universe shrinks in size. So a very long time ago the whole of the universe was squeezed into an unimaginably small and dense grain of matter, no larger than the nucleus of an atom. The universe must have arisen from a 'singularity', a unique event that cannot be fully described by the laws of physics. The standard theory asserts that the universe had an 'edge', an absolute beginning and that science cannot fully get back to this initial singularity, as the laws of physics and relativity are suspended in the primeval fireball. This point would be unimaginably hot and dense. At 't = 0' about fifteen billion years ago this incredibly dense pinhead of energy 'exploded', expanding rapidly and violently, creating space and time. As it expands and cools, small variations in the density of matter lead to the formation of stars, galaxies and planets including the earth. Gradually the force of gravity slows the expansion of the universe. The conclusion that we can draw is that our universe is not eternal; it has existed for a finite amount of time and so had an absolute beginning. It is enormous in scale, continually expanding at speeds approaching the speed of light at the edge. Because of its size, it is very old.

What will be the fate of the universe? A clear conclusion of cosmology today is that, though the universe is very old, it will not last forever. The fact that the mutual gravitational attraction causes the expansion to slow down suggests two possible future scenarios: the universe is either open or closed. It will either collapse in on itself (the 'Big Crunch') or keep expanding away to infinity, all the time getting colder (heat death). Everything depends on how much matter there is in the universe. If there is enough matter, the pull of gravity will overcome the expansion and the universe will begin to contract and eventually implode in a 'Big Crunch'. This is the *closed* model of the universe. Another possibility could be the so-called 'Big Bounce'. As a result of the violent compression of the universe into this singularity, there could be another 'Big Bang' with a new universe being formed, from Big Crunch to Big Bounce where everything will expand again. But in an *open* universe, if the total mass of the universe is less than the critical mass, expansion will continue indefinitely dissipating energy and ending in a 'heat death'. Present observations suggest an open-expanding universe as the actual mass of the cosmos falls short of the critical mass. A complication may be the existence of hidden or 'dark' matter as estimates vary and it is not clear if there is sufficient mass to bring about the ultimate collapse of the universe. An open or flat universe is the more likely theory given our present knowledge. The universe is expanding from a state of hot density to a cold void; the farther it expands, the lower will be its temperature and the more extensive its decay.

Cosmology and creation

These discussions about the origin of the universe inevitably raise fundamental religious questions. The root metaphysical question is: does the cosmos result from a cosmic accident or a purposeful Creator? Does the universe arise from blind chance or purposeful design? Big Bang thinking has raised in a new way the question of the relationship between religion and science. Thinking about the beginning and end of all things cannot avoid raising questions about God. What are the theological implications of modern cosmology? Many religious people welcomed Big Bang Theory as supporting and confirming the Biblical doctrine of Creation. The claim of modern cosmology to have discovered an absolute beginning of the universe at $t = 0$ would appear to have a direct religious implication. If the universe had a beginning would it not mean that the biblical account of creation in Genesis makes scientific sense? How better than through the doctrine of creation and the idea of a Creator God could we explain the mysterious event of how the cosmos came into existence so abruptly out of nothing? Has the book of Genesis found conclusive support in the new cosmology? The idea of a 'free lunch', whereby once nothing exploded into everything, goes against the expectations of science. In science based on causal explanations, nothing comes from nothing. Big Bang would seem to suggest that God is the one who set the original boundary conditions, who brought time and space out of nothing. Robert Jastrow claims that Big Bang cosmology has bridged the worlds of the Bible and science, and that the astronomical evidence leads to the biblical view of the origin of the world. If the universe is not eternal, it has not existed forever; does it not require a transcendent cause?

The well-known physicist Stephen Hawking writes that the concept of an absolute beginning suggested in the standard Big Bang model implies the existence of a Creator. The notion of a beginning means that there is an 'edge' to the cosmos and that raises the question about what is beyond the edge. Hawking does not want to admit this, so he proposes a hypothesis to eliminate the edge; he challenges the claim that there once was a singularity prior to the big bang. It does not imply an 'edge', an initial singularity, a beginning of time. If the universe is completely self-contained, having no boundary or edge, it would have no beginning moment, it would simply be. For him, it is possible to imagine time as gradually emerging out of space so that there may well have been no clear first moment, and so no first cause either. His quantum cosmology claims that space-time arises by chance out of a more simple state. Hawking sees the theological implications in his negative answer to the question: what place then for the Creator? Peter Atkins agrees that modern cosmology renders the motion of creation by God superfluous. In a self-contained universe without boundaries and initial conditions the Creator would have no job to do. So here we have two diametrically opposed theological interpretations of modern cosmology – for and against a Creator.

It is hardly surprising that theology is very wary of attempting to draw theological conclusions from cosmological discoveries. It is very important not to equate 'origins', the beginnings of the cosmos in science with the act of 'creation' by God. Even if the world never had a beginning, a first moment in time, we could still believe it was created. The theological understanding of creation is not just about beginnings, as we have seen in 2.4, but about the world's ontological dependence at all times on God. Whether the universe had a beginning in time or is eternal is irrelevant as in either case it requires a transcendent grounding in order to sustain it in existence. The crucial point to appreciate is that the Christian doctrine of creation is about agency. Creation is an act of an *agent* God, causing things to be rather than not be (existence), whereas Big Bang and other cosmological theories are about the *mechanisms* by which the world came to be. They answer fundamentally different kinds of question. Cosmology answers *how* things came to be, whereas creation answers *why* the world exists rather than not existing at all. Christians have no difficulty in accepting that 'Big Bang' was the mechanism, the process by which the world came about, while still holding that God was the agent of creation.

It is a form of 'category mistake' to claim that the *act* of creating has not occurred because we have explained the *process*. Many popularisers of science promote the idea that scientific explanations of origins displace divine agency and purpose; this is to confuse two different kinds of question. Scientific method, based on observation and experiment in the material universe, can neither deny nor affirm the existence of a Creator God. God lies outside the boundary of scientific inquiry. No scientific theory can explain how something came out of nothing; this is beyond the realm of science. Creation *ex nihilo* is a religious explanation that cannot be demonstrated by science. The concept of creation is not to be identified with any particular scientific theory of origins. Albert Einstein said that the only thing that is unintelligible about the universe is that it is intelligible. Cosmology raises 'limit questions' concerning the intelligibility of the cosmos, questions that arise in science but cannot be answered within science itself.

The new view of the cosmos does have positive theological implications: it raises in a new way the most fundamental question of all, the question of contingency, why is there something rather than nothing? The contingency of the universe, the fact that it does not have the reason why it exists within itself, is a fruitful area for the conversation between science and religion today. Contingency, as the non-necessary existence of the universe as a whole, requires an explanation. Theology sees the answer in *creatio ex nihilo*, the freedom of God to create; he might have chosen differently, no world at all, or a world with different laws and initial conditions. So various scientific descriptions of the origins of the cosmos are compatible with an understanding of God as creator. To say that God is the creator is to say that the existence of the universe depends for every moment of time on God. Creation is not at the beginning – that is the question of origin; creation is now and always. Creation is not self-explanatory; it is not self-sufficient. But how and when it came to be is a matter for science to work out. These initial conditions of the universe raise intriguing religious questions summed up in the notion of the 'Anthropic Principle', to which we now turn.

The Anthropic Principle

The universe has a biography, a story of life, and a narrative with a beginning, a middle and an unknown end. We are becoming aware that our planet is just one tiny part of the great story of the cosmos. Being puny, conscious creatures in a vast mindless universe suggest to scientific materialists that we are 'aliens', accidental by-products of blind evolutionary processes. But cosmology today tells a different story. The remarkable claim is made by modern physics, that the evolution of human mind and consciousness may be what this universe is all about. To think of life as somehow fundamentally a part of the universe, as opposed to being some accidental by-product, is the claim of the Anthropic Principle.

The term is used to refer to the remarkable 'fine-tuning' of the early universe in giving rise to human life. 'Anthropos' is the Greek word for 'human'. A striking discovery of modern cosmology is that there are certain basic features of the universe, which have enabled living organisms, and ultimately human life, to develop. The physical conditions that enabled life to exist are very sensitive to a small number of fundamental constants. If the values of these constants had been only slightly different we would not be here, life would not have evolved. The universe seems 'fine-tuned' to our being here. Science has discovered that the conditions for life seem to have been woven into the fabric of things from the beginning.

What are the cosmological constants that are fined tuned to the production of life? The overall chemical composition of the universe was determined by the first few seconds of the Big Bang. The elements on which life depends (such as carbon, oxygen, nitrogen and iron) are the product of nuclear reactions within stars. In both cases the processes by which the elements are formed are governed quite precisely by the strength of four basic physical forces:

Gravitation – long distance attraction between masses.
Weak Nuclear – responsible for radioactive decay
Strong Nuclear – binds quarks together in protons and neutrons.
Electromagnetic – responsible for light and the behaviour of charged particles.

If the relative strengths of these forces were only a little different, the universe would be very different or non-existent. If you were to make gravity a little stronger or weaker than it is; or if you changed the mass of the electron in its electric charge; or if you make the nuclear reaction within stars a little more or a little less energetic; or if you altered the violence of the Big Bang, in any of these cases, life would not happen.

Among the remarkable fine-tuning features are the following:

1   *The formation of elements:* In the crucial first three minutes,
    the gross nuclear structure of the world was fixed as a
    quarter helium and three-quarters hydrogen. Tiny
    variations in the forces would change everything. If the
    strong nuclear force had been only slightly stronger, the
    world would be all helium; no hydrogen means no stars
    would have formed, no water and hence no life. If the force
    had been slightly weaker, hydrogen would dominate; no
    helium means super-novae stars would not explode and so
    not eject the heavier elements into space such as carbon,
    nitrogen and oxygen, which are necessary for life. Carbon is
    made within the giant nuclear furnaces of stars over
    thousands of millions of years. Our bodies are composed of
    carbon, the 'ashes' from long dead stars.

2   *The expansion rate:* There is a very critical balance between
    the outward explosion of the Big Bang and the pull of
    gravity drawing things together again. If the rate of the
    expansion had been infinitesimally greater, the universe
    would have expanded too rapidly for stars and planets to
    form and there would only be empty space; if the rate were
    infinitesimally smaller (by one part in a thousand million),
    the force of gravity would collapse the universe before it got
    going. Either way we would not be here. The expansion rate
    depends on size of the initial explosion, the mass of the
    universe and the strength of the force of gravity.

3   *The matter/antimatter ratio:* The laws of physics suggest that
    matter and antimatter in the early universe should have
    cancelled each other out. But in fact there was an excess of
    matter over antimatter of one part in a billion. For every
    billion antiprotons in the universe there was one billion and
    one protons. The billion pairs wiped each other out
    producing radiation, leaving just one proton over. A greater
    or smaller number of surviving protons, or an equal

number, would mean there could be no material universe. If the laws of physics are symmetrical between matter and antimatter why was there a tiny asymmetry here, which produced our universe?

The simultaneous occurrence of so many improbable coincidences at the Big Bang means that the cosmos seemed to be balanced on a knife-edge. Reflection on how the extraordinary initial conditions of the universe appear to be fine-tuned for intelligent life has led some cosmologists to formulate the 'anthropic principle.' It is popularly called the 'Goldilocks Effect' from the fairytale. It highlights the fact that the conditions for humans to exist, like Baby Bear's porridge, chair and bed, are 'just right'. The number of things that had to come out just right for us to exist is immense.

There are weak and strong versions of the anthropic principle:

- Weak: if the fundamental constants of the universe were different, we would not be here, life would not have evolved
- Strong: the universe contains within itself the potential for life, such that it was impossible for human life not to have developed.

The principle underlines the importance of the observer, in the formulation of Dickie and Carter: 'What we can expect to observe must be restricted by the conditions necessary for our presence as observers.' The evidence for 'fine-tuning' has been the subject of considerable discussion among scientists, theologians and philosophers.

The Anthropic Principle and religion
What, if any, is the religious significance of the anthropic principle? The coincidences are fascinating and thought-provoking and have led some scientists to propose a religious

explanation. The remarkable features of our universe suggest something like design, meaning or purpose. The weak version seems to be a statement of the obvious, that conditions are just right for us to be here, and we can observe only what the conditions that produced us allow us to see. But the strong version implies that the whole evolution of the universe took place in the way that it did just *in order* that human life should appear. The universe must have those properties that allow life to develop within it at some stage in history; so the vast construction of the cosmos exists simply for our sake. The whole universe right from the beginning must have been orientated toward the existence of conscious minds, like the initial conditions of the acorn seed is orientated toward growth into an oak. The important conclusion is that conscious beings are not 'aliens', the product of the blind evolution of matter, but are an inherent part of nature. The anthropic principle is a protest against the reductionist view that tries to explain the more (mind and consciousness) in terms of the less (matter).

Some have seen this fine-tuning as evidence for cosmic design, for the existence of a designer God. Stephen Hawking wrote that the odds against a universe like ours emerging out of something like the Big Bang are enormous and may have religious implications. Freeman Dyson argues for design and claims the amazing coincidences of physical constants that have produced us seem to suggest 'the Universe must have known we were coming'. The cosmic fine-tuning is claimed as evidence that the universe was designed to permit the evolution of life forms. Does the strong anthropic principle provide a new form of the Design argument for the existence of God? From the perspective of Christian faith, the fine-tuning of the physical constants could be seen as confirmation of religious belief, as it is consistent with the existence of a purposeful Creator.

Theologians are cautious about taking the anthropic principle as evidence for a designer God, or in placing human beings in a privileged position within the universe. The principle seems too 'anthropocentric', too narrowly focused on human existence. We have learned from experience how mistaken it is to base religious claims on the shifting sands of scientific theories. History teaches that arguments from design have later turned out to have scientific explanations. As we have seen, Newton had a designer God to explain the workings of the universe, but he proved to be vulnerable to the 'God of the gaps'. Paley's argument for the design of human bodies was overturned by Darwin's evolution by natural selection. The Strong Principle is an example of 'conflation' of religion into science, the confusion of theology and science, to attempt a scientific validation of God; there can be no demonstration for the existence of God from science. Physics cannot tell us anything about our reason for being here or about the world's meaning.

The anthropic principle highlights the direct link between the emergence of human life and the size and age of the universe. The cosmos needs to be the size and age it is for us to exist. But these immensities do not mean we are lost and insignificant in a pointless universe. A very old expanding universe has to be a huge universe. The fifteen billion year history of the expanding universe has produced more and more complex and organised structures, especially on our tiny planet and the process is still continuing. The simplest atoms of hydrogen and helium formed clouds of gas that condensed into galaxies and stars. Stars grew and collapsed; in their death throes giving rise to more complex systems like carbon. At a later stage still, planetary systems were seeded with carbon atoms, and on our planet complex molecular structures gave rise eventually to the evolution of life and consciousness. The chemical elements in our bodies were forged in the furnaces of stars. Physicists have calculated that the time it would take for self-conscious agents to evolve from simple atomic structures would be about fifteen billion years. The conclusion is inescapable: the universe needs to be just about the great age and size it is, if humans are to evolve according to the basic laws of physics. It turns out that humans are not peripheral to the universe after all, even if we are dwarfed by the enormity of cosmos. Consciousness and complexity are more important than sheer size. Life is not just an accidental by-product on an unimportant planet in an insignificant galaxy. It is part of the constituents of the universe.

Cosmology teaches the interdependence of all things, that the cosmos is all of one piece and that we are part of a much larger community of being. Humanity is the most advanced form of life we know, but it is part of a wider process in space and time. Biological evolution is only a tiny part of cosmic evolution; we are the late arrivals in the evolutionary story. Humans recapitulate in themselves the history of cosmic evolution. We carry in our physical structure, in our genes and molecules the history of our ancient past. It is human minds that understand the workings of the cosmos and, to some extent, they can begin to change and control it. Humans are that part of the universe that has come to consciousness of itself; the universe has come to self-awareness in human beings. This is a very different picture from the dualism of Descartes who saw humans as spiritual substances dropped as strangers into an alien material universe. By contrast, cosmology today sees us as parts of a continuum of increasing complexity in the material order; we are part of the comic process, that part which has self-awareness. We can begin to understand our own nature and so shape it ourselves.

It is hardly surprising then, that the focus of recent discussion in religion and science has shifted away from evolutionary biology and toward the bigger picture of cosmic evolution and the physics of the early universe. Given the initial conditions and the cosmological constants, it is not unexpected that evolution would eventually produce conscious life. There is an emerging sense in biology and cosmology, against materialist and reductionist views, that the material cosmos is not the enemy of life and mind but that the latter were already latent in the fine-tuned early universe.

In summary, the fine-tuning of the physical constants has led many cosmologists to raise questions as to whether the cosmos had a designer God. The existence of God cannot be proved by these coincidences, as there is always the possibility there may be other explanations. For religious persons, who believe in God for other reasons, the anthropic principle confirms and strengthens their conviction that the theistic explanation is the best one. It is more reasonable to think that the universe originates from a purposeful Creator than from blind chance.

Two ancient contrasting cosmologies

As long as humans are on this earth they have been preoccupied by the question of origins. Tribal religions told stories of the origin of the universe and life on earth. Creation stories serve a very different function from scientific theories. The Native American origin story called 'The Earth on the Turtle's Back' relates how a piece of mud placed on the Great Turtle's back became the whole universe. The story is told, not as a scientific picture of beginnings, but as a response to the need to understand human life within a larger context of meaning and order. These stories provide a cosmic framework of meaning and so give some practical guidance for living in a web of relationships with others and the world of nature. We will examine two ancient cosmologies: the Babylonian Myth and its relation to Genesis and the world-view of the ancient Greeks.

The Babylonian Epic and The Book of Genesis

The Babylonian creation story *Enuma Elish* is part of the ancient literature of Mesopotamia (modern Iraq), which may have inspired the Biblical texts of Genesis on origins. The story, written in the twelfth century BCE, retells the ancient myths of creation, the flood and the events that led to the building of Babylon as home for the gods. The struggle between cosmic order and chaos was, for the ancient Mesopotamians, a fateful drama ritually played out at the beginning of every year in order to assuage the fears of the people faced with the forces of disorder. The poem starts with the primeval watery chaos and the monsters of chaos. The cosmos unfolds through conflict among the male and female deities in the heavens. The creator god Marduk fought Tiamat, the goddess of the sea, who represents the forces of chaos and malevolence. Having slain her, he divided her body in two and with one half he formed the sky and with the other he formed the earth. He put bones and blood together and made humans to become slaves to perform the menial tasks for the gods. Marduk is elevated to chief of Babylon and to foremost among the pantheon of the gods because of his role in creation, and builds a Temple to himself.

Enuma Elish is often compared to the creation account in Genesis. There are similarities as well as significant differences between this Babylonian myth and the Biblical stories of creation. The Genesis stories freely used the symbols and metaphors drawn from the common eastern cultural setting to affirm their own distinctive view of God and creation. The two stories of creation in the opening chapters of the Book of Genesis are very different. The first is the carefully structured creation of the world, and the different kinds of creatures, within the framework of seven days (Gen 1:1-2:4) and is called the 'Priestly' narrative. It was written about six centuries before the birth of Christ, a time when the people of Israel were in exile in Babylon, with the intention of counteracting rival, pagan Babylonian stories of origin. The second, the story of Adam and Eve in the Garden of Eden, focuses on the creation of humans, and the entry of sin into the world (Gen 2:4-3:24). It is a far older story, written in the tenth century BCE and is known as the 'Yahwist' narrative, because it uses the distinctive name of 'Yahweh' for God. We will concentrate on the first, leaving the Yahwist story to our discussion on creationism later in the chapter.

The Priestly account is primarily concerned with the ordering of the elements of the universe and portrays the great cosmic sweep of God's work in creation. 'In the beginning God created the heavens and the earth' (Gen 1:1). The whole universe and everything in it is created by God's word alone as an ordered cosmos. The first act of God is the pronouncing of his word: 'Let there be light'. Words express thoughts or intentions so God's word states his divine purpose in creating. In the Priestly account the order of creation in six days was as follows: the first three days God divided light from darkness (first); the dome of the sky separating the waters below the heavens from the waters above (second); the dry land from the sea (third). There followed three days of filling the void with the sun, moon and stars set in the dome of the sky (fourth); the sea creatures, fish and the birds (fifth); the land animals and finally humans (sixth). Humans are God's masterpiece in creation. Being made in God's 'image and likeness' highlights our spiritual awareness, that we are capable of relationship with God. Humans are entrusted with moral responsibility and are to be partners with God in caring for the earth and not exploiting it. They are given the gift of being 'like God', of being able to know and love God their Creator and Father and of entering a relationship with him. The first origin story finishes with the picture of God 'resting' on the seventh day, the 'Sabbath' day, setting it apart as a holy day, a day of rest from toil, a day to contemplate the works of God, the beauty of his creation and to delight in it. The whole poetic account leads to the joy, rest and peace of the Sabbath.

The main aim of the Priestly story is to make clear that creation is the work of one God and that it is good. There are no battles in the heavens among the deities as in the Babylonian myth. Creation is not the outcome of conflict among the gods but takes place simply through God's sovereign word of command. The world and the heavens are not full of deities and demons. In fact, the so-called gods like the sun, the moon and the stars are really creatures in the service of the one and only God. God is transcendent to the created world, which is not made from any pre-existing materials or from the bodies of the gods, but when God speaks his creative word. The original chaos is a common feature to both stories. 'The earth was without form and void and darkness was on the face of the deep.' (Gen 1:2). The dark void of the sea is the symbol of chaos, the formlessness that threatens the order of creation. But God through the power of his spirit shapes and forms and brings order out of the world of chaos. Creation is orderly and planned, resulting in a harmonious and interdependent whole. In the Babylonian story, human beings were created to provide slaves and playthings for the gods. According to Genesis, they derive their dignity as children of God made in the divine image, endowed with the gift of freedom and made for relationship with him. So Genesis, while acknowledging the limitations of the authors and the cultural influences of their time, is fundamentally different from these other creation stories. It affirms the transcendence and sovereignty of God and the dignity of humanity. The Bible is inspired by a monotheism rather than by the polytheism of Babylon; it promotes moral behaviour and attitudes rather than magic, sorcery and superstition. The Biblical Creator creates humans in his image for a purpose that is both moral and spiritual: as steward of God's creation and as doing God's will in relationship with him.

How are we to understand the Genesis story today and how does it relate to modern scientific cosmology? It is important to understand the hermeneutical issue at stake here. This means interpreting correctly the ancient texts of Genesis, revered by Jews and Christians as the inspired Word of God, by attempting to discover what questions they were meant to answer in their own time and context. They were not written to answer scientific questions of how the world came to be. They were composed in story form to teach profound spiritual truths about how people ought to live in relation to God, to others and in harmony with the earth. What the Bible provides is a sacred cosmology, a spiritual interpretation of the world's origin, nature and destiny and not a scientific cosmology. The opening chapters of the Book of Genesis are an imaginative poetic account, a symbolic portrayal of the fundamental relationships between God, the world and humans. These poetic stories assume a pre-scientific cosmology of their time, but we today can separate the enduring religious meanings from the ancient cosmology in which they were expressed. That cosmology was based on the earth in the centre of a three-tiered universe, with heaven above and hell below. A similar worldview was shared by the Babylonians and by many peoples of the ancient world. The cosmology of the Biblical authors has no authority for religious believers, as these ideas are not compatible with modern science. What the Bible reveals are religious meanings, the truths of our salvation, not ancient science or cosmology. The Bible teaches some fundamental theological truths that we can still accept independently of any scientific cosmology, ancient or modern.

What are the theological insights that are communicated in the Biblical narratives? Firstly, God the unique Creator is transcendent, sovereign and free and pre-exists his creation. God wills the creation and acts in an intelligent, purposeful and ordered way. Secondly, the creation has an on-going relationship of dependency on the Creator. Thirdly, the world God creates is essentially good and blessed. God delights in his creation. Humans have a special place, created in the image of God, have the gift of freedom and are morally responsible for their actions. These are basic religious insights about God and the world valid at every moment in time, and not statements about events in the past. There is, then, no incompatibility between the Genesis story of creation and modern Big Bang cosmology as they answer fundamentally different kinds of question. As we have seen, creation is about *agency*, the unique action of God bringing things into existence. Big Bang is a scientific theory about the *mechanism*, the process by which the world came to be the way it is.

Ancient Greek cosmology

The ancient Greeks took it for granted that the universe is eternal and uncreated. The great Greek philosophers Plato and Aristotle held that the world had no beginning and will have no end. Plato pictured a realm of eternal forms and timeless truths, imperfectly reflected in the sensible world around us. To understand the real, according to Plato, a person has to look beyond the flawed, ever-changing world of experience, which is only an imperfect copy of the most perfect, universal and unchanging world. There are two very different worlds: the world of Forms, ideal, perfect and unchanging, and the imperfect changing world of our everyday experience, full of growth and decay. Aristotle took a different view, that our knowledge of the world begins with sense experience interpreted by our reason. Yet, Greek ideas on perfection and imperfection were central to Aristotle's view of the cosmos. For Aristotle the alternative, that the world had a beginning in time, was unacceptable as it violated the principle that something could not come from nothing. The cosmos did not come to be and cannot cease to be. Aristotle's view of an eternal, uncreated universe would prove troublesome for Medieval Christianity's view of the cosmos as God's creation. The Greeks were the first to construct a model of the cosmos in which to interpret the motions of the sun, the moon, planets and stars. Aristotle saw the eternal cosmos as a great sphere, divided into two distinct regions, the upper region of the perfect, unchanging heavens, and the lower region of the changing, imperfect earth at the centre. Motion in the heavens is uniform, circular motion, so the seven known planets in their spheres moved in perfect circular motion around the earth. The stars were fixed on the outer sphere, which rotated about the earth once every day (See 2.1 on Aristotle).

For Aristotle, motion is never spontaneous as there can be no movement without a mover. The heavenly spheres are composed of 'quintessence' and their motion is eternal and perfectly circular. What is the cause of this movement in the heavens? Aristotle proposes a 'mover' that is itself 'unmoved'; otherwise there is an infinite series of movers. He called the unmoved mover of the planetary spheres the 'Prime Mover', a living deity who represents the highest good, outside the planetary spheres at the outer limit of the cosmos, beyond the sphere of the fixed stars. God is not the creator of the material world, but only the cause of order and motion. He is pure thought, a rational soul contemplating and knowing itself alone, and has no knowledge of the world. How, then, does the Prime Mover cause motion in the heavens as there is no contact between mover and moved? God was not the efficient cause of the world (the agent that created it) but the final cause (the purpose or goal towards which things tend). This means that the Prime Mover is the object of desire for the heavenly spheres, which try to imitate its unchanging perfection by performing eternal, uniform circular motions. In fact, Aristotle identified a number of Unmoved Movers, one for each of the heavenly spheres as the final cause of its heavenly motion. He thought that these divine spirits were the cause of motion as they impelled the planets to seek their natural purposes or ends. This was the cause of movement, without which everything would be at rest.

Aristotle attempted to describe the cosmos, not simply as it is, but as it must be of necessity. The cosmos is necessary because it could be deduced from first principles, without much reference to observation and testing. Though he believed that all knowledge begins with sense experience, he developed his system largely upon deductive reasoning. True knowledge was grasped in universal definitions, which could be of use as premises in deductive demonstrations, like a proof in Euclid. Once you grasped the essential composition of the heavens and the earth, then certain things followed with regard to their respective motions; it could not be otherwise. The heavens were perfect and unchanging, so motion had to follow a perfect form, that is the eternal, repeating motion of a circle.

Aristotle's natural philosophy proved to be an obstacle to the rise of science for two basic reasons. Firstly, a necessary world deduced from first principles discovered by reason, from the top down, did not require detailed observation and experiment to discover what it was like. Any observations that contradicted reason must automatically be wrong. Secondly, Aristotle's preoccupation with teleology, with purpose and the final causes of things, hindered the scientific approach based on physical laws and quantitative measurements. His primary goal was to understand the 'essential natures' of things. Aristotle thought that all change and motion could be traced back to the natures of things. In his scheme of Four Causes, Aristotle gave priority to the final cause, to the role of purpose in his universe. The cosmos is not a place of chance but an orderly, organised world, a world of purpose in which things develop toward their proper ends determined by their natures. By discovering purpose you can deduce what a thing is made of and how it works. An acorn becomes an oak tree because that is its nature, the end toward which it is moving. Aristotle did not have the modern scientific interest in quantitative relationships between things. Galileo showed that falling rock is better explained in terms of physical laws, like gravity, than in terms of its essence or the final cause of motion.

The ancient Greeks saw the world in a more mystical way, permeated by mind or soul, which accounted for its order. Matter appeared to possess mystical qualities, endowed with tendencies to certain kinds of change and motion. Mysterious intelligences were at work moving the planetary spheres and encouraging things to seek their natural goals or ends. The world was regarded as an intelligent organism, based on the analogy between the world of nature and a human individual, and because it was in constant movement, it was taken to be alive, like an organism. Such views could lead to pantheism, that the world was semi-divine; this would have a negative effect on experimental science, as it would be sacrilege to interfere with a sacral world. In the seventeenth century, Newton's alternative model of a mechanical universe drove the spirits out of the universe and opened the way for a world that worked on purely mathematical principles. Descartes, with his division between mind and matter, claimed that the material world contains no unfathomable mysteries that are not transparent to reason. Nature could be understood mathematically without any reference to purpose and final causality. This is not to say that there is no Final Cause, but only to exclude God from the scientific level of explanation.

Some contemporary contrasting cosmologies

We shall examine two quite different and contrasting cosmologies, one based on the latest scientific theory, Big Bang; and the other is a religiously based scientific view called Creationism, which is based on a certain interpretation of the Bible as science.

Big Bang/Flaring Forth

In the nineteenth century scientists considered that the Newtonian mechanical paradigm gave a complete description of the physical world. It was thought we live in an unmysterious, mechanically determined, law-abiding and predictable world that is basically simple in its structure right through to the atomic level. The twentieth century ushered in a radically new understanding of a changing and expanding universe, described in the standard Big Bang Theory or the 'Flaring Forth' as it is technically known.

The foundations of Big Bang theory go back to Einstein's theory on general relativity. His theory of General Relativity (1915) was a radical theory about gravity, which related time, space, mass and energy in a series of equations. For Newton, gravity was a force exerted between masses as they moved about in space. Einstein argued that gravity is a distortion of space and time, the 'curvature' of space-time. What determines the curvature of space-time? The structure of space-time, its size and shape depends on the distribution of matter, while the motion of matter is determined by the curvature of space-time. 'Space tells matter how to move; matter tells space how to curve'. A visual image may help to shed light on all of this. We could visualise space-time as a stretched rubber sheet. Placing a heavy ball on the taut sheet, where it makes a large indentation, can simulate the effect of a massive object in space. Small objects, like marbles, moving along the sheet, follow curved paths, because of the distortion made by the heavy object. This curving of their trajectories corresponds to the force of gravity. As space stretches, so does time. Time passes more slowly where there is less gravity and space is also elastic, being compressed as gravity increases.

Einstein accepted the common scientific view of the time that the cosmos was eternal and static, and that the basic structure of matter remained unchanged forever. The universe is the same as it has always been. In 1917, a Dutch physicist Willem de Sitter, while working with Einstein's recent equations on general relativity, concluded that they implied a changing and expanding universe. A Russian mathematician Alexander Friedmann also realised that Einstein's equations challenged the idea of an eternally unchanging universe. Einstein himself realised there was a real problem in reconciling general relativity with a static universe. If the universe were eternal and static, the various masses would by now, under the force of gravity, have collapsed upon one another. Newton's solution was to employ God to keep the stars from gravitational collapse and from clumping together! But a changing and expanding universe implied that it must have expanded from a singular initial point in the past, a starting point that was unacceptable to Einstein and to the scientific community generally. He responded by introducing a controlling 'cosmological constant' into his equations. Some constant force inherent in the cosmos, he speculated, kept the stars apart and the universe from collapsing and also from expanding. No one questioned this, as there was as yet no real observational evidence one way or the other, for a changing universe or for one that was always and forever the same.

Gradually experimental evidence accumulated that the universe was indeed expanding, as predicted by Einstein's theoretical work on relativity. Gravity is a distortion of space and time in general relativity. His special theory described the world as a single four-dimensional 'space-time continuum'. Time is inextricably bound up with space. The importance of this is that the big bang explosion was the origin, not only of matter, but of space and time as well. As space stretches so does time. The expanding universe is not seen as matter exploding through empty space; rather, space itself is stretching and inflating bringing the galaxies with it. If the big bang saw the creation of space it also marked the beginning of time. There was no time before the big bang because there was no 'before'. The point from which the present universe expanded out in a colossal explosion of energy and heat is termed a 'space-time singularity'. It is a point from which space and time have come, not a point within space and time. Here the analogy with an explosion breaks down; in the latter, matter is flung outwards to fill the surrounding space. In the big bang, space and time are created simultaneously with that event. It was the expansion of space itself, from nothing, that was responsible for the expansion of the universe. The galaxies are not speeding away from us through space; it is better to think of them as being carried along in the tide of continually expanding space in the aftermath of the big bang. It is like being in an expanding bubble where the bubble is everything and there is nothing 'outside' the bubble.

Contemporary cosmology and high-energy physics combine to give us a plausible reconstruction of cosmic history, beginning with events three minutes after the big bang, when protons and neutrons combined to form nuclei. Five hundred thousand years later, atoms were formed. One billion years from the beginning, galaxies and stars were being formed, and then planets at ten billion years. At twelve billion years, microscopic life forms appeared on our planet earth, and biological evolution got under way. The last quarter of a century has seen a refinement of the theory of an expanding universe. The farther back we go before the three minutes, the more speculative are the theories, because they deal with states of mass and energy in extreme conditions. Recent interest has centred on 'Planck time' 10^{-43} (ten million, billion, billion, billion, billionth of a second) as a fraction of the first second of the universe's history, when the whole universe was the size of an atom and affected by quantum theory. This is the frontier of our knowledge, the current limit beyond which we cannot go with present theory. Big bang refers to the age of the universe from about one ten thousandth of a second onwards up to about a half a million years, when atoms were formed from electrons and nuclei. In standard big bang theory, $t=0$ is a singularity at which the laws of physics do not apply. It would have been a dimensionless point of pure radiation of infinite density.

There are essentially three kinds of evidence for the big bang:

a. The Hubble constant: In the nineteen-twenties the American astronomer Edwin Hubble was instrumental in showing that the Milky Way galaxy was just one among many others and that the universe was much bigger than anyone imagined. In 1924, he noticed that light coming from distant galaxies was 'redder' than light from nearby galaxies. This could only mean that the light waves are longer than normal and that the source of the light must be moving away from the observer. This can be explained by comparison with the Doppler Effect in sound: the pitch of a train whistle changes as it approaches and then recedes from the listener, as the frequency of the sound waves are shortened or lengthened out. There is similarly a relationship between the frequency of light waves and the relative speed of the stars: light from stars moving towards us is 'blue-shifted', whereas light from those moving away from us is 'red-shifted'. The best explanation for the red shift is that the galaxies are receding from the earth and from each other at enormous speeds. Hubble noticed there is a proportional relationship between the speed of recession of a galaxy and how far it is. This is his famous Hubble Constant of 1929, which states that the further away a galaxy is the faster it is moving away. The speed of a receding galaxy is proportionate to its distance from us. The inescapable and most startling conclusion is that the universe is expanding in all directions. If it is expanding, then it must have been in a more compact state in the past: it must have had a beginning.

Hubble's discovery was so surprising and unexpected that many were very sceptical, if not downright incredulous. Why was the universe expanding? But there was already a complete theory to describe the behaviour of an expanding universe, Einstein's general theory of relativity. Observational astronomy was now beginning to confirm the expanding universe predicted by Einstein's equations. Hubble's evidence of expansion compelled Einstein to abandon his model of a static universe. Einstein's theory did indeed agree with observation. From the speed of the expansion, it is possible to calculate the age of the universe. At an earlier time in history, the galaxies must have been closer together. If we go back further, the universe seems to be expanding from a common origin, a 'hot bang' about fifteen billion years ago.

b. *Background radiation:* Further evidence came in 1965 when the American astronomers Robert Wilson and Arno Penzias detected cosmic background microwave radiation coming from all directions in space, the 'afterglow' of an initial hot bang. Their discovery was one of those happy accidents that can occur in science. They picked up a faint hiss on their radio telescope coming from all parts of the sky, which they could not explain, and interpreted it as a fault in their equipment or even pigeon droppings in the bell of the telescope! The full significance of their discovery emerged when others had predicted that the big bang would leave a trace of itself as microwave radiation spread evenly across the sky. A blinding flash of light accompanied the big bang, like any explosion. The cooled down remnant of that flash remains as a faint hiss coming from all directions, left over from the hot stage. The background microwave radiation at about three degrees above absolute zero (-270 C) was found throughout the universe. This uniform background radiation was the best evidence to date that the universe had a beginning in a singular cosmic event about fifteen billion years ago.

The discovery of the background radiation made possible other evidences for the big bang from theoretical and experimental work in high-energy physics. From the present temperature of the background radiation we can compute how hot it has been in earlier stages. The reason for this is a calculation that as the universe expanded it cooled, as it doubled in size it lost half its temperature. Using modern particle accelerators scientists can recreate conditions at earlier stages of the universe and have been able to simulate the heat of the initial explosion. In the simulated small-scale big bang it is possible to work out what proportion of different kinds of atom were present in the original big bang. It turns out that the proportion of hydrogen to helium was seventy-five to twenty-five per cent, exactly as it is today. There is no particular reason why it should be so unless it was fixed in the beginning. Big bang theory, then, explains a present day occurrence that would otherwise be inexplicable.

c. Cosmic ripples: One of the difficulties with Big Bang was that it failed to explain how galaxies were formed from a smooth, uniform beginning. Big bang implied that the universe emerging from the initial expansion would be smooth and uniform in all directions. We know we live in a 'lumpy' universe today: the cosmos is made up of unevenly distributed matter with galaxies, and dense clusters of galaxies in some places and seemingly immense empty space in others. If the universe began with a smooth big bang, how did it get so far from that uniform distribution of matter today? At one time all the matter in the universe was spread out uniformly as a hot gas that has gradually cooled in the expansion. How do you get from light gas to heavy elements like stars and galaxies? To produce all the irregularity the universe must have had the seeds of such unevenness at the earliest stages of its development. Where was the evidence of this 'lumpiness' in the form of variations of the temperature in the background radiation? We have already seen the temperature is the same everywhere; about 2.7 K (-270 C). Big bang theory could not take the lumpiness of the universe into account, that is until recently.

In 1992 data collected from a NASA satellite COBE (Cosmic Background Explorer) detected tiny variations in the background radiation at a very early stage of the universe. There were minute differences in the density of matter in the early universe, which is exactly what is needed to explain the birth of galaxies. There were 'ripples' in the radiation out of which later forms of matter evolved; these were the seeds of the uneven universe we know today. Lumpy matter pulled together and heated by gravity forms stars and galaxies. The COBE results removed another obstacle to the big bang.

Steady state versus big bang
The strength of the big bang model of scientific origins is the breadth of its explanatory power. It integrates and links together different areas of scientific inquiry from cosmology, astrophysics, geology and evolutionary biology into a coherent framework. The universe has an amazing history, a long story to tell, beginning with the fireball, expanding and cooling, forming stars and galaxies, our sun, the planet earth and eventually life on earth.

For many physicists the idea of big bang was abhorrent and they resisted it both on scientific and religious grounds. The big bang is a singularity, a point at which the laws of physics break down; as we approach the singularity at t=0, gravitational forces, temperatures and densities increase without limit. The initial conditions and the initial starting point are without precedent and without cause, and therefore seem outside scientific study. An axiom of modern science is that every physical event can be explained in terms of preceding physical causes. Big bang suggested that everything came from nothing in a once-off event, a singularity; this goes against all expectations and appeared to many scientists as irrational and untestable. What is also unexpected is that an ordered cosmos could come from a chaotic explosion. The affront to science in big bang theory is that matter is not eternal and so the universe should not have existed.

An alternative theory was proposed, to explain the expansion of the universe and to avoid the big bang, by the British astronomer Fred Hoyle in the nineteen fifties, called 'Steady State' theory. Against big bang, the theory states that the universe is infinitely old and it was not evolving or changing through time. It held that the expansion of the universe is constant. As the universe expands, new matter is created so that its density remains constant. The outward movement of the galaxies was balanced by the continuous creation of matter throughout space. Matter was 'popping' into existence from time to time to keep the cosmic density constant. This model avoided the notion of a beginning by putting forward an infinite time-span. The task of physics was to discover how the expanding universe brought new matter into existence to balance the outward movement. Both big bang and steady state theory agree on an expanding universe; they differ on how to explain the phenomenon. Steady state required the continuous creation of matter to produce new galaxies as the universe expanded, whereas big bang proposed that all matter was present from the beginning.

Hoyle's steady state theory had a wider cultural appeal in the fifties in a world recovering from war and in the shadow of the atomic bomb. A universe that has gone on forever and is steadily creating itself has more consoling and peaceful overtones than the unsettling one that begins with a violent explosion from nothing. There were many flaws to the model, such as the failure to explain the continuous creation of matter or to account for the chemical composition of the universe. It was eventually abandoned in favour of big bang after it could not account for background microwave radiation. Though it was Hoyle who disparagingly coined the phrase 'big bang', yet there is a broad acceptance today of the standard big bang theory for the origin and structure of the world, a theory which is compatible with the best available evidence.

The conflict between the two theories was at the time seen as a battle between religion and atheism. The initial singularity of the Big bang was very congenial to a theological interpretation, as it appeared to affirm the Genesis story of creation. A universe that begins with the big bang appeared to be friendlier to the religious story of creation in Genesis than an eternal cosmos. Some claimed that modern cosmology had made creation intellectually respectable as science had 'found God'. How better could we explain the coming into existence of the universe from nothingness than by the doctrine of a Creator God? The astrophysicist Robert Jastrow argued that 'the astronomical evidence leads to a biblical view of the origin of the world'. Such ideas, which linked big bang with creation, were unacceptable to many scientists who were atheists. Such scientists preferred the steady state model as they presumed it got round the creation problem. If the universe is as it has always been, then there has never been a first moment, a starting point. Hoyle admitted that he favoured steady state not just on scientific grounds, but also because it was more compatible with his own atheist beliefs and furthest away from the account of Genesis. Others got around the problem of the world having a beginning by favouring an oscillating universe. This proposed a succession of big bangs alternating with big bounces in order to hold onto the claim of an eternal universe.

The debate helps to illustrate the fact, already mentioned, that we should not draw theological conclusions from scientific theories, such as equating big bang with creation. The stories of creation in Genesis have nothing to teach science about cosmic beginnings. Neither is it the business of science to deal with ultimate questions. Whether the universe had a beginning (big bang) or not (steady state), it would still require a creator God. The question of creation is about the ontological dependence of everything that exists on God. There is no scientific theory of the origins of the universe that is more favourable than any other to the notion of a Creator; on the other hand, there is no scientific theory that can rule out a creator. In the words of Michael Poole, 'science can neither confirm or disconfirm a Creator'.

The universe implied by relativity and big bang cosmology is neither eternal nor necessary, but radically finite. But a finite universe is a contingent universe, that is, there is no necessity for its having come into existence, or for its being the way it is. If this particular universe need not be here at all, as science states, then it is a legitimate question to ask *why* it exists if it did not have to. The new scientific picture of the universe compels us to re-ask in a dramatic way the age-old question: why does the universe exist rather than not exist at all? Why does it have the physical laws it has rather than any other? Science cannot answer these 'limit' questions about the ultimate ground of the being of the world or about the ultimate meaning of the universe. The interplay between modern cosmology and religion emerges in such limit-questions that arise in science but cannot be answered within science itself. The scientific sense of wonder at the amazing story of cosmic origins is at least open to a theological interpretation. Though the scientific search for beginnings is a very different question from the religious question of creation, nevertheless they both come from the fundamental human concern to discover our roots.

Creationist cosmology
A key issue for religious believers in assessing scientific theories, like cosmological origins and biological evolution, is the nature and the authority of the sacred texts that underpin their beliefs. For Muslims, the question is how should science relate to the Qur'an, understood as the literal spoken words of God, the absolute truth, which must therefore be taken seriously by scientists. For Jews and Christians, who share the Hebrew Scriptures, the question is how are we to interpret the Bible, especially the key texts on origins in Genesis. Among Christians, there is a broad consensus that Genesis is a symbolic and poetic story that teaches a religious message about the fundamental and enduring relationships between God, the world and human beings.

On the other hand, some conservative Christians today take their stand on the literal truth of the Bible, since the Bible is the divinely inspired Word of God and is inerrant in every detail. Biblical literalists argue that if there is a conflict between the letter of the Bible and modern science, science must be wrong as the Bible is always right. This would rule out the scientific story of origins, biological evolution, and the origin of life. Many fundamentalist Churches in the United States, like the Southern Baptists, maintain the inerrancy of the Bible and a literal interpretation of Scripture. 'Fundamentalism' arose as a religious reaction to the rise of secular culture within American Protestantism in the nineteen-twenties, centring on their total opposition to evolutionary theory.

The 'warfare' idea was reinforced by the celebrated 'Monkey Trial' in nineteen-twenty-five in Tennessee. A teacher John Scopes was prosecuted for teaching Darwinian evolution when state law permitted only the biblical account of creation in the curriculum. The law passed in Arkansas in 1928, to prevent the teaching of evolution in public schools, was in 1968 overturned by the US Supreme Court because it was deemed to be unconstitutional.

'Scientific creationism' or 'creation science' goes back to that time, the late sixties and seventies when some scientists, who were also fundamentalists, tried to circumvent the court ruling by arguing for equal time of creation science with evolution in public schools. Instead of arguing against evolution on religious grounds, like the older fundamentalism, that it is anti-biblical and anti-religious, creationists claimed that evolutionary theory is bad science. For creation science, the Bible is a textbook of *science* and provides a better scientific account of origins than evolution, which is only an undemonstrated theory and not fact. It is important to note that creation science, though founded on religious grounds from a literal interpretation of Genesis, is put forward as a *scientific* theory. It contains no explicit reference to a creator God but claims to give the most reliable scientific information as an alternative to evolution by natural selection. One of the foremost exponents was Henry Morris who developed the arguments in his *Scientific Creationism* written in 1974 and in later publications.

What are the central tenets of creation science? The Bible, as a book of science, is anti-evolutionary in two basic claims: 'special creation' and a 'young earth'. It is convinced that evidence in geology and biology supports the biblical picture rather than evolutionary theory. The word 'creation' in creation*ism* is used in a particular way to mean 'special creation'. God created fully formed creatures, in many separate acts, and not through a slow, gradual evolutionary process. 'God created everything according to their *kinds*' in Genesis is interpreted to mean 'fixed species'. All species of living things were more or less fixed at the moment of creation, and any changes in life forms since have occurred only within very narrow limits. They did not evolve over long periods of time. A large gulf exists between humans and other species as human beings are specially created. The lack of transitional forms in the fossil record implies for creationists that Genesis is a better account than Darwin for the origin of the species. The young earth creationists see the six 'days' of Genesis as twenty-four hour periods when the cosmos was created. The earth is less than ten thousand years old and a catastrophic flood accounts for the geological features on its surface. The cosmos only appears to be old and was created fully developed, so cosmic evolution is also rejected as big bang cosmology is flawed and unproven. Surveys show that forty-five per cent of Americans believe in the special creation of humans within the last ten thousand years. Creation science wants to preserve the uniqueness of human creation and the direct intervention of God to bring it about.

Creation science harks back to an older nineteenth-century biblical literalism; with the exception that creationism is stripped of all reference to biblical events (garden of Eden, Noah, the deluge, etc.). Creationists reject great tracts of established science, in cosmology, physics, biology and geology in the name of the science in the Bible. In 1987 the US Supreme Court struck down a creationist act in Louisiana that required creation science be given equal treatment with biological evolution in public schools. The court judged that creation science supported a particular religious view and so violated the separation of church and state.

Creationism is a protest against the worst excesses of secular modernity strengthened by the evolutionary world-view. Creationists understand evolution as a closed materialist philosophy involving the rejection of God and a sense of the sacred. It stands for a degrading view of the human as a savage beast, a breakdown of moral authority and a loss of values. If that is their judgement, then it is understandable that great energy is spent in keeping evolution out of schools and textbooks and in promoting an anti-materialist view based on

Genesis as science. The literal interpretation of the Bible is seen as the one rock of absolute certainty, defending traditional values and human dignity in a time of social breakdown and moral confusion. Creationism has a point as a reaction to the ways evolutionary theory is sometimes popularly and erroneously presented as an anti-religious reductionism. Extravagant claims are often made for evolution, which is often presented with an anti-religious bias, as if materialism or atheism is an objective conclusion of biology.

Difficulties with creationism

How are we to regard creation science? For the majority of scientists, as well as Christians, creationism is fundamentally flawed. Critics accuse it of not being legitimate science at all. Creationism shows nothing of the rigorous method of science, in the latter's dedication to evidence gathering, observation and experimentation. The scientific evidence in favour of evolution is cumulative and impressive coming from a whole range of disciplines, from geology, palaeontology and radio carbon dating to genetics. Modern genetics has solid evidence to show that living species are closely related, sharing genes that perform similar functions in very different bodies. Species are not as different from one another as creationists claim. Furthermore, appealing to a Creator who created a fixed nature in a unique act at the beginning of time is outside the canon of scientific inquiry.

For many Christians evolution is compatible with creation but not with creationism. Creationists assume that evolutionary theory is incompatible with Christian faith. This is a false dilemma, that one must choose between science or religion, evolution or a literal interpretation of Genesis. Many Christians take creationists to task for their hermeneutical principles, on their literal interpretation of Genesis. Genesis is the word of God for Christians and is revered for its insights into God's revelation. The creationists treat the Genesis texts as a source of scientific information. This ignores the historical and cultural context of their origins, their theological meaning and their non-scientific intentions. These texts were composed in a pre-scientific age and reflect the pre-scientific speculations of the ancient world. There is a wide diversity of literary types in the Bible, from historical, symbolic, poetic, devotional to mythical and other kinds of material. Creationists fail to distinguish between them when they seek contemporary scientific theories in passages of the scriptures. It is not the task of religious accounts of creation to present details about the physical origins, the mode and the timing of the beginnings of things.

The stories of Genesis have nothing to do with cosmic beginnings; as we have already said, creation is about the ontological dependency of all that exists on God. Hence, creationism diverts attention away from the deeper theological meaning of the sacred texts, expressed in symbolic and poetic language. Genesis is a symbolic portrayal of the basic covenant relationships between God, humans and the created world. The universe is God's gift and is a good and ordered world, a place where humans can relate to God with gratitude and trust in his providence. These religious meanings can be separated from the ancient cosmology in which they were embedded. Creationists miss the real intentions of the Genesis text and address the wrong questions to it when they look for scientific theories there. Genesis attempts to shed light on the big questions of life, the questions of meaning and purpose. Religious symbols convince us that life makes sense in terms of an ultimate frame of reference, in terms of the ultimate mystery of the universe.

3.2   THE NEW PHYSICS AND RELIGION – EMERGING QUESTIONS

The new physics began with the discoveries of relativity and quantum mechanics. As we have seen, relativity theory showed that the physical laws operate within local and limited conditions. If we consider space, time, gravity and mass from the point of view of an observer on planet earth, then Newtonian physics works well. We still need to do Newton-style calculations to send a rocket into space to escape earth's gravity. Once we look at the universe on the large scale and the forces at work, where gravity warps both space and time, then Newton is of little use. Special relativity led to the startling situation that the presence of an observer is inseparable from the scientific description of the cosmos. The observer's position and velocity are crucial with respect to the concepts of simultaneity and the measurement of mass, length and time. Quantum theory further boosted the contribution of the observer and undermined the deterministic picture at the sub-atomic level.

Quantum theory and Heisenberg's Uncertainty Principle

The idea that matter is made up of very tiny indivisible particles or 'atoms' separated from one another by empty space is an ancient one, going back to the Greeks of the fifth century BCE. The idea of atoms as invisible, irreducible things of which all substances are composed has a long history in the West and was accepted by scientists like Boyle and Newton. Until the discovery of the electron in 1897, atoms were thought to be indivisible little solid globes, like billiard balls. The atom was then discovered to have a nucleus, comprising protons and neutrons, with electrons circling round it. Niels Bohr produced a model of the atom in which negatively charged electrons orbited the positively charged nucleus, the way the planets orbit the sun. Matter is therefore far from simple; it is composed of complex arrangements of nuclear forces, binding together particles, some divisible into smaller particles called 'quarks'.

Quantum physics gives a subtle account of the small-scale structure of the world today and has been a source of much controversy among scientists since the 1920s. It posed problems of interpretation that are still with us in the claim it appears to make that nature is indeterminate and unpredictable. The major new development came in 1900 with the German physicist Max Planck and his basic idea of quantum physics. In classical physics, light consists of a continuous stream of particles, forming a string of energy. He discovered that radiation (e.g. light or energy) was seen as coming, not in a continuous stream, but in small packets or 'quanta', hence the name 'quantum theory'. A source of bewilderment for physicists was to think of entities such as light as being both particle and wave, sometimes showing one face, sometimes another. Under certain circumstances light can behave in a particle-like way rather than in its usual wave-like way. It flew in the face of common sense and classical physics to hold that light was both particle and waves. There appeared to a great ambiguity or paradox at the heart of the quantum world. The energy given by the light is packaged in a way that is related to the frequency of the wavelength rather than spread evenly over the wavelength. The relationship between the energy a quantum carries and its wavelength depends on what is known as the Planck constant. The amount of energy in each quantum increased as the wavelength of the radiation got shorter.

In the nineteen-twenties physicists developed a complete theory of quantum physics (or quantum mechanics), based on the idea of wave-particle duality. One way of thinking about wave-particle duality is to say that a quantum entity such as a photon or an electron travels as a wave but arrives as a particle. Erwin Schroedinger formulated the wave equation of quantum mechanics, which accounts for the energy levels of electrons in atoms. But the equation does not refer to the location or trajectory of an electron; it refers to *probability*, the probability of finding an electron in one location rather than another. Quantum mechanics cannot predict the action of individual particles, but describes the atomic world in terms of probabilities, based on the observation of very large numbers. This is similar to an opinion poll, which can predict how a population will vote, but is unable to be precise about the way any one individual will do so. Quantum physics deals with probability rather than with individual certainty at the atomic level. The Bohr model of the atom, based on planetary motion, with an electron flying round a nucleus is highly visible; but the electrons in quantum mechanics could not be pictured at all. The quantum world is a much more indeterminate and insubstantial world than that of classical physics.

One of the great pioneers of quantum mechanics was Werner Heisenberg. He was convinced that the nature of the quantum world imposed strict limits on the accuracy of what could be measured. The very act of measurement somehow interferes with what we are trying to measure. Uncertainty is a basic implication of the quantum world. In 1927 he formulated his Uncertainty Principle which states that the more accurately we measure the *position* of an electron or other particle, the more difficult it is to measure its *momentum* and vice versa. It is impossible to know both at the same time. Position and momentum are paired up in quantum theory; when we attempt to be more precise in our measurement about one, then we are less precise about the other. In dealing with particles, it appears that their behaviour is random; they are not 'caused' like events on the larger scale. Uncertainty characterises other pairs also, such as time and energy. We can predict when half of a large number of radioactive waves will have disintegrated, but we cannot predict when a particular atom will. We can predict only the probability that it will disintegrate within a given time interval, it could be in the next minute or in a million years. The Uncertainty Principle is crucial for understanding the quantum world.

The Principle raised very fundamental questions concerning the interpretation of a world that displays uncertainty and unpredictability at the sub-atomic level. In the world of classical physics there is no incompatibility between measuring the position of an object and the speed at which it is travelling; but in the quantum world there is. Quantum uncertainties generated an intense debate among physicists concerning the nature of the real world. In particular, it posed a philosophical problem concerning the relationship between measurement and the real that is measured. The debate centred on whether uncertainty is the result of the way we examine nature, or whether it belongs to nature in itself. Is it that we have not yet developed the correct technique for the simultaneous measurement of the position and speed of a quantum entity, or is uncertainty a property of nature itself and so it will always be impossible? Einstein rejected indeterminacy in nature and was convinced that the uncertainties of quantum theory are due to our present lack of knowledge. Quantum mechanics is an incomplete description of reality. Order and predictability would eventually be found in the sub-atomic world as in the larger world. He famously said 'God does not play dice', rejecting the idea of random happenings and indeterminacy in nature. Heisenberg was convinced that indeterminacy is truly an objective feature of the natural world and not a limitation on our knowledge. Quantum mechanics is about statistics; it deals with the world of probability waves. It is the nature of an electron not to have a definite position but its possible positions are spread throughout the wave. Observing consists in compelling one of the many possibilities to actualise itself, the wave function collapses into the one value that is observed. The future is not simply unknown, it is not yet decided. More than one alternative is open and there is room for spontaneity and novelty. There seems to be an intriguing interplay between law and chance.

Quantum physics, then, raises basic issues of the relations between law and chance, part and whole and the observer and the observed. Quantum mechanics implies a new role for the observer and a new kind of relationship between the observer and the world observed. Cartesian dualism separated the physical world from the mind of the observer. In quantum physics the observer is not just a neutral spectator but also a participant in the interactive process. Niels Bohr said that in the drama of life we are players as well as spectators. For him, we cannot visualise the world as it is in itself, apart from our interaction with it. The quantum world exists more as possibility than as actuality. The presence of the observer contributes to the movement of the quantum world from possibility to reality, in the collapse of the wave function to having one value. Whatever we observe, we influence. The observer actually brings about what is being observed. Subjectivity has entered physics; the observer is part of the observation. There can be no sharp distinction between the observer and the observed as stated in classical physics.

Chaos theory and complexity

Chaos Theory, with relativity and quantum mechanics, is the third contribution to the paradigm shift from the deterministic world of classical physics to the new physics of the twentieth century. Quantum mechanics states that there is real randomness about the behaviour of sub-atomic particles and so prediction can only be in terms of probabilities. The acceptance of quantum uncertainties helped scientists to accept a degree of openness and unpredictability about the physical world at the level of everyday things. In 1903 Henri Poincare was the first to notice the great sensitivity of many physical systems to small variations in initial conditions. Scientists have become gradually more aware of both 'chaos' and 'complexity' in the behaviour of the physical world, helped by powerful modern electronic computers. Chaos theory studies the mathematics of hypersensitive systems, that is, the ways in which very small and unpredictable disturbances in one place may trigger a sudden and dramatic change in another. Complexity looks at the ways in which nature has a tendency to produce more and more complex organisms by the application of a few basic rules. Examples of complexity would include cells, organisms, brains and ecosystems. Chaos looks at complex phenomena that are non-linear and appear to be beyond the grasp of timeless, deterministic laws, such as the weather, the shape of clouds and the dynamics of flowing fluids. Scientists speak of the 'butterfly effect' to illustrate how sensitive many natural processes are to their initial conditions. A minute fluctuation at the beginning of a hurricane, such as the beating of a butterfly's wings, may influence its shape or trajectory. The poet Francis Thompson hints at the idea: 'thou can'st not stir a flower without disturbing a star'.

If prediction and control are central to science then chaos casts doubt on their applicability to many processes in nature. The word 'chaos' here does not simply mean disorder or randomness, but scientists use it to describe the complex patterns that arise surprisingly out of turbulent situations. The world is full of surprises: complex order can arise 'spontaneously' out of chaos and apparently simple ordered processes can suddenly give rise to chaos. A natural process may begin simply, then it may become turbulent and chaotic, but then unexpectedly emerge into beautiful, complex patterns of order. There is 'order in chaos', as underlying the chaotic behaviour there are often geometric forms of order. Patterns called 'strange attractors' limit the range of the chaotic processes and pull them toward unexpected and intricate order. Order emerges spontaneously in complex systems, especially on the border between order and chaos. Too much order makes chaos impossible; too much chaos makes continuity impossible. Dynamical systems represent a 'structured randomness' in the world. The science of complexity and chaos are revealing a universe that unfolds in the shape of self-organising systems, which adapt themselves to the natural world. The universe tends towards diversity, unpredictability and complexity. Chaos and complexity are signs of an unfinished world, open to novelty and surprises.

Theological perspectives on these developments

Theology today must speak about God's relation, not to an ancient or medieval or Newtonian world, but to the dynamic, emerging, self-organising world that develops through the interplay of law and chance. What are the implications of quantum mechanics and chaos theory for the interplay between science and religion? Understandably many theologians and scientists are wary of attempts to find theological meanings in contemporary physics, from which God is methodologically excluded. Nevertheless, relativity, big bang, quantum mechanics and chaos theory have fundamentally altered the way we see the world today. The picture of the universe we have today is that of dynamic interplay between the physical laws and the contribution of chance. Chance is not an alternative to law but the means whereby law is creative, allowing for the genuinely novel and the unpredictable.

Quantum indeterminacy and theology

Does the new physics have any theological implications, either positive or negative? The notion of indeterminacy in quantum mechanics has been to the forefront of many recent discussions in science and religion. For many materialists, quantum indeterminacy and chaos theory is evidence for a purposeless universe, the product of randomness and chance. Randomness and chance challenges the idea of divine purpose in nature and any sense of meaning, purpose or value. Chance accounts for everything and supports a scientific materialism in which matter is the fundamental and the only reality. Our existence is the product of pure chance and not divine purpose. As we have seen, according to Richard Dawkins and the Neo-Darwinists the presence of chance means we live in a purposeless universe. Chance and necessity together are the mechanisms that explain everything and there is no need for God. This is the reductionist point of view, in which the whole is merely the sum of the parts.

We are 'nothing but' the molecules, atoms, and sub-atomic particles of which we are composed. If our constituent particles behave in a random fashion, then we as a whole are the products of chance, lacking any overall meaning and purpose.

But quantum mechanics challenges, not only the determinism, but also the reductionism of classical physics. The holistic character of quantum physics means that reality cannot be analysed as the sum of its separate parts, the whole is greater than the parts, and this is a principle that underpins reality. Reality is seen as a complex entity in itself, rather than in its parts. Holism promotes a multilevel view of reality and the emergence of new kinds of events at higher levels of organisation. A 'one level' view of the physical universe does not fit an emerging universe with different and irreducible levels of complexity and order. The structure of the material universe displays a hierarchy of complex interactions, each level building on the levels below, but the higher is not reducible to the lower. The whole person can neither be analysed nor adequately understood in terms of some or all of the parts of the human personality (see 4.1).

For many theologians, the new physics is interpreted to be more congenial to the place of human freedom and divine agency in the world than the rigid determinism of a mechanical universe. The question of divine action, how God acts in the world he has created, has received particular attention in the light of the new physics. We have seen how God was progressively edged out of having any function in the physical world as scientific explanations replaced the 'God of the Gaps'. Darwin's theory dismissed the idea that individual living creatures were the immediate products of divine design. The Christian tradition sees God as actively sustaining the order of the physical universe, that God continues to sustain the laws that govern the regularity of the cosmos.

A recent positive theological response to quantum indeterminacy is to claim that it reveals a world open to divine agency. God not only sustains the laws and the regularities of nature, but he also works through the openness and indeterminacy of the natural world. Some theologians maintain there is compatibility between quantum theory and divine agency. This is not a completely determined world, but one in which the laws and processes God has created can give rise to novel structures through the operation of chance. Real freedom in God and humans requires an open future. Quantum physics is interpreted as providing this openness to the future with Heisenberg's notion of ontological indeterminacy, that it is a real objective feature in nature. Quantum indeterminacy, thus, provides the 'causal joint' on this account of God's action. Without interfering with the laws of physics and without being scientifically detectable, God is understood as the determiner of indeterminacies at the quantum level because of the 'gappy' nature of the system. God determines what actual value is realised within the range of a probability distribution; it is God, not the human observer, who collapses the wave function to a single value. Quantum indeterminacy provides the 'window' for divine action in that God influences some quantum events.

Many scientists and theologians are unhappy with this theological interpretation of quantum mechanics. A difficulty with this position is that it confuses a gap, something missing in the ontological structures of the system, with indeterminacy, the openness of natural systems to a variety of outcomes. In principle there are no gaps in the universe, which is complete at its own level. Also, because it does not allow for God's action at higher levels, from the top-down rather than from the bottom-up. Quantum influences work 'from below', whereas organic influences work 'from above', at the macro level. Others emphasise that a better way to go is to think of God as creating the processes which *themselves* can, sustained by God, give rise to novelty, diversity and complexity.

Chaos and complexity and theology

What is the contribution of chaos and complexity theory to the science and religion debate? Some sceptics interpret the theory to exclude a religious interpretation of the universe. Chaos gives rise to order spontaneously, and so there is no need for an external supernatural designer to bring order out of chaos. Matter's capacity for self-organisation renders superfluous the idea of an ordering deity. For many scientists and theologians today, the opposite is the case in that chaos and complexity provides a powerful critique of the materialism and reductionism based on linear systems. In scientific materialism a combination of blind chance and physical necessity explained everything. This picture is no longer sustainable because chaos and complexity means we do not have to choose between a rigid determinism or a blind randomness. We can never specify fully the initial conditions in a natural process that would enable us to predict completely its future state. An indeterminate universe, where intricate patterns of order arise out of non-linear chaotic processes, is open to novelty and surprises. Chaos and complexity are signs of an unfinished world.

Theology sees a coherence between the emerging scientific picture of chaos and complexity and the creative God who is the ultimate source of novelty and surprises. In an emergent, open universe God is continuously sustaining the universe in every moment and actively guiding the way it develops. In an unfinished world, God is at the heart of the evolving process empowering it from within and guiding it toward eschatological completion. Divine providence is compatible with the real randomness in the world and this compatibility in turn can shed light on the incomprehensive, gracious mystery of God. Theologians are attempting to construct a new theology of nature that will integrate the new view of the universe comprised of complex, chaotic and evolutionary systems with belief in the creative and promising God of religious faith. Why is our universe evolving from simplicity to complexity? How is it that the random quantum processes of the early universe have produced order and stability? How has a simple universe produced higher and higher levels of complexity? There are two extreme positions that are difficult to reconcile with religious viewpoint. The total determinism of a mechanical universe excludes God, as does a world of pure chance that operates in completely random fashion

The new cosmic story

Christian theology has the task of reflecting on the story of the universe told by contemporary science and engaging with it. One of the great scientific discoveries of the twentieth century, the expanding universe, affirms that the universe has a history. The past has been radically different from the present in the sense that the universe did not come into being ready-made and complete; rather it has and continues to make itself through a long evolving history, from simplicity to increasing complexity, through the interplay of law and chance. The unimaginably long history of the cosmos from the Big Bang to the present and the still evolving galaxies, as well as the evolution of matter on earth from non-organic to living things, and from simple life to human consciousness, is a story caught up in the subtle interplay of law and chance. We humans are the universe become conscious of itself. The universe is a gradually unfolding process and that process is fundamentally irreversible. If we were to roll back the clock to a time before life on earth and then let it roll forward again, would we humans appear as we are today? Science is unanimous in saying no, so multiple and diverse are the variables that combined to produce our species. The 'arrow of time' is only in one direction and the script is not written in advance. The universe has a narrative, elements of biography, and a story of life.

The universe story is much bigger and more extensive than our human story. This is bound to affect our view of God and his purposes in creation. It is not as if God spent billions of years biding his time for conscious beings to appear who could enter a dialogue with him. From the beginning, God delighted in the beauty and diversity of a self-organising universe for its own sake, and not only for its value as a backdrop to human life. We do not live at the centre of the universe, yet God has written into the fabric of the creative process the delicate balances between law and chance, which has enabled conscious minds to emerge from matter, minds who seek to understand the process by which they came to be.

The potentiality of matter, the complexity of self-organising systems, the unpredictability of evolution, the interplay of law and chance, the presence of chaos and novelty and the multi-layered processes of the world in becoming raise questions about our idea of God and his action in such a world. For John Haught, it is only because of God's self-emptying love (*kenosis*) that a self-organising universe can come into being. The new scientific picture of the world can help deepen our understanding of God, who is not outside (Deism) but is within, deeply involved in the creative processes. Randomness, uncertainty and indeterminacy in nature are what are required by a loving God. Love does not compel or control, so if God loves the world he gives it a certain freedom or autonomy to be itself; God 'lets be'; he creates a world distinct from himself, something other than God. God's persuading love allows for an unfinished world, full of uncertainty, randomness, experimentation, adventure and risk. God's self-denying love wished to share his divine creative life with all creation, to be partners with him in the on-going drama of the long struggle of the universe to arrive at life, consciousness and human culture. In the words of John Polkinghorne, 'God did not make a ready made world... he created a world able to make itself'.

The contemporary theological response to the scientific picture of the universe today could be summed up as 'holistic thinking'. The totality of creation, with all its great richness and diversity, is a unified whole grounded in one creator God. The one God creates the whole cosmos as one diverse but interrelated system. He lets it be itself but he is present in every part of the cosmos sustaining and empowering it from within. The evolutionary history of the cosmos reaches its goal in God's self-communication through grace to human beings and through them to the whole universe. This same loving God will bring the whole evolving creation to completion in an unknown future.

Select bibliography

Barbour, I. *When Science Meets Religion*, London: SPCK, 2000

Haught, J. *Science and Religion: From Conflict to Conversation*, New York: Paulist Press, 1995

Morgan, J. *Born with a Bang: The Universe tells our Cosmic Story*, Nevada: Dawn Publications, 2002

Stannard, R. *Science and Wonders: Conversations about Science and Belief*, London: Faber and Faber, 1996

Swimme, B. and Berry, T. *The Universe Story: From the Flaring Forth to the Ecozoic Era*, San Francisco: Harper, 1992

Ward, K. *God, Chance and Necessity*, Oxford: One World, 1996

4

Current Issues for Religion and Science: Life and Death

4.1 THE LIFE QUESTIONS

Opposing views of the human being

Two very different and opposing views of the human being are worth introducing. They can be described as Scientism or the Scientific Reductionist viewpoint and the Personal or Religious viewpoint. Both claim to be scientifically credible and both have many adherents from within the scientific community. In outlining these theories one confronts core differences between an atheistic and a theistic view of human nature. One also sees the manner in which science is used, for the most part illegitimately, in an attempt to bolster the credibility of either viewpoint.

The Scientific Positivist view of the Human Being

The atheistic ideology of Scientism or Scientific reductionism as opposed to the academic discipline of science is a most important philosophical challenge to religion. It is an atheistic theory that owes its origins to the eighteenth-century Scottish philosopher, David Hume, for whom the 'self' is only a stream of consciousness. What we experience are thoughts, feelings, memories and emotions, but we don't experience a separate entity called the 'self'. What followed was a reductionist view of the human being as a machine, a grouping of chemicals, a system of engineered bones and sinews, 'a pack of neurones' (according to Francis Crick, one of the discoverers of DNA) held in a working harmony for the period of life. Death marks the break-up of the unity, the disintegration of the different elements, and the dissolution of the human being. The soul, consciousness, thought, feeling and the whole realm of the spiritual is no more than 'the froth on the beer' – an 'epiphenomenon' or a by-product of material interactions. Human nature, its intelligence and its feeling is *no more than* its neural, biological and genetic make-up. Francis Crick's famous 'astonishing hypothesis is that "You", your joys and your sorrows, your memories and your ambitions, your sense of personal identity and free will, are in fact no more than the behaviour of a vast assembly of nerve cells and their associated molecules...'. This is the classic statement of Scientism or Scientific reductionism.

Reductionism means that the lower explains the higher, the simpler explains the more complicated, and the foundation explains the structure. There is nothing wrong with it as a scientific method: fundamental particles explain physical matter and energy, chemical interaction explains biological life, utility and value explains economic choice, and so on. But it is one thing to use a method to reduce something to its basic elements, and another to say that the elements are the only essentials. Can we say 'The heart is just a blood pump', 'The mind is only a computer', 'The human body is simply a machine', even though the analogies of pump, computer and machine explain a lot about the way the body works? If we answer 'Yes' to that question, then we are promoting Reductionism; we are claiming that science tells us everything about the human. A Christian can and does respect Reductionism as a scientific methodology, but cannot accept it as the entire measure of what we know. In a way, scientific reductionism is a 'Lego' view of the universe (meaning the children's plastic building blocks which can be assembled into immensely complicated fabrications). Reductionism succeeds by viewing a thing only in terms of the components that make it up. The cake is only its recipe. The poem is simply the alphabetical letters. The symphony is purely the individual notes. If you divide the components into the entire reality, you have explained it all with nothing left over, with no remainder, as they say.

The last human mystery for scientific reductionism is consciousness: our subjective sense of being somebody. Scientists have made great strides in explaining much about intelligence and emotion, especially with the research known as 'artificial intelligence', which tries to duplicate with a computer the activity of the human mind, and with the practice of drug therapy whereby emotions and feelings can be changed by mind transforming chemicals. Scientists who subscribe to the atheistic ideology of scientific reductionism believe that sooner or later they will be able to adequately describe, and satisfactorily explain, consciousness. They argue like this: 'Chemicals alter the way we think and feel; therefore, the way we think and feel is chemical.' The brain is known in computer circles as 'wet ware', and intelligence is described as 'band width'. The belief in the possibility of producing a computer with consciousness encourages scientists of a reductionist frame of mind to hope for complete success sometime in the future.

The religious idea of the human being

The Personal and Religious view (especially in its Christian version) insists that there are two dimensions to the human being, the spiritual and the material. The human being eats and thinks, is rooted in the here and now, the concrete circumstances of the present environment, and also is capable of abstract thought, creative imagination, eternal longing, and enduring relationships. In other words, the human being seems to exist in two realms: the material and the spiritual. In the Christian view, spiritual is an adjective, not a noun. There is only one being with two aspects. We are not bodies, with something else, called a soul, added on. The dualism of Plato thought of a human as a loose juxtaposition of two opposing substances, a material body and a spiritual soul. The soul is the real *you*, which happens to be temporally attached to imperfect matter which will disappear at death. In the Christian tradition, you don't have a body; you *are* your body. We are composed of two co-principles that belong together in the unified human being. We are beings with a material and an immaterial side to us, and human beings relate to both realms: the earthly and the spiritual. To speak imaginatively, human beings exist on a horizon between the world of spirit and the world of matter.

The Biblical concept of the human being was clearly neither dualist nor reductionist. For the Hebrew Bible (the Christian 'Old' Testament) the human is a unified being. The book of Genesis says that God 'breathed into the man the breath of life and man became a living being'. The Biblical writer makes use of the popular image of the life as breath, but takes the extraordinary step of making it God's breath. The man has the divine life within him. The first chapter of Genesis has an even more extraordinary image: 'In the image of God, God created him; Man and Woman, God created them'. The human being is already part of a purpose and a plan. Human beings, from the start, exist in a relationship with each other and with God.

What is a 'Person'? A person is a being with consciousness and freedom. (The early theologians used the terms 'intellect and will'.) Another way of putting it is that a person is capable of awareness and responsibility. This definition leaves personhood open for infants (who cannot yet be aware or responsible) and disabled or sick or injured people (who may not be functioning as aware or responsible at the moment, but could, at some time in the future, or did, at some time in the past, exercise these qualities).

To be a person is to be 'constituted by meaning'. Human beings recognise their location in the world, their relationships to others, to their own past, present, and destiny, and then acknowledge their duties and obligations in the light of their awareness. On being born, an infant is, at once, a member of the human race (with every other human, living and dead), of a community group, of a family, and, in the mind of Christians, a child of God. In other words, the person is relational. The most important aspect of a person is relationship with others and with the world and with God. The person becomes conscious and aware of these relationships, and thus, of the obligations and responses that these relationships demand.

To sum up: Reductionism regards the human being as entirely material: a mechanical and chemical construction that will not survive its disintegration. From the religious perspective of a Christian, the human being is personal, relational, social and responsible, spiritual and material, individual and communal, temporal and eternal.

The beginning and end of life

The contribution of Charles Darwin is crucial to understanding modern scientific theories on the origins of life. In essence, in the spirit of scientific reductionism, Darwinism attempts to remove all consideration of purpose and design from the story of the origin of life. Where previous generations had found it impossible to see how inanimate matter could generate the organisation and direction and self-generating energy that accompanies any sign of life, Darwin's theory of natural selection seemed to suggest a way in which randomness and chance could result in some order and vital activity. Even though this is a questionable hypothesis, nevertheless it is one that remains core to the philosophy of contemporary Neo-Darwinists, as we have seen in 2.3. Evolution depends on chance, competition and cruelty with the apparent elimination of purpose, direction, and the intervention of a loving God.

Thus, from the perspective of scientific reductionism as enunciated by contemporary Neo-Darwinists, evolution is interpreted as leaving no room for the belief in a creator God. As Richard Dawkins recently remarked: 'Darwin made it possible to be an intellectually fulfilled atheist.'

Although it flies in the face of the reductionist claims of Neo-Darwinism, many scientists who are theists can and do accept some form of evolution theory as a stepping stone in the search to understand the origins of life. They see it as a way of understanding God's creative process that respects the on-going nature of creation. The apparent randomness and probabilities discerned in nature reveals a purpose and direction behind or beyond nature that respects the complexity and the beauty of God's creation. The apparent chance and randomness emphasised by evolutionary theory incorporates a freedom and lack of determinacy into the universe and in history, which leaves events open-ended and unrestricted. This, strangely enough, allows for success and failure, grace and sin, comedy and tragedy, and for the affirmation of hope and the love of God in a way that a fully determined and certain chain of cause and effect would scarcely permit. Furthermore, it leaves room for human beings to recognise their dignity as partners and co-creators of the universe with God. The cosmos is not a finished project with humans present simply as passive spectators. Humans have the real possibility and indeed the responsibility to shape the world in a manner that respects the delicate ecological balance that has evolved over billions of years.

In the final analysis, theists and in particular Christians want to assert the creation of the universe by God, not because it provides an explanation for the origin or start of everything that they would otherwise lack – cosmology provides that – but because it explains something else entirely, namely, the ontological dependence of the world on God and his continuing presence in it as he guides it to completion. It gives an answer to the question of the future rather than the past. Where is the universe going?

What is the destiny of the human race? What is the meaning of each individual human being? Should we experience our lives as joyful or sorrowful? Is there reason for hope? The belief in the creation of the universe, and the individual creation of each human being by God, affirms that life is meaningful both for the species and for the individual. It assures us that the future holds promise of salvation no matter how desperate the situation may be. It announces that a relationship of love for fellow human beings, care for creation, and respect for the Creator is fundamental to existence. In this context, the appropriate Christian response to Scientific reductionism is one that draws attention to questions concerning the future of the cosmos and the human race rather than those that over-emphasise problems surrounding the origin of the species.

Fundamental issues
Discussion of current issues for religion and science such as those relating to our understanding of life and death inevitably raise issues concerning the scope of human stewardship. Are there limits to human stewardship of creation? How are these limits set? By appeal to reason, human rights, religion, 'God's law', the 'common good', nature?

The scientific endeavour pushes towards practical products. 'If we can do it, then we must do it'. Or at least, we ought to try it. Ethics (philosophical and theological) on the other hand, has a much wider point of view. It raises the 'ought we do it' question. There may be 'forbidden knowledge', things we can do, but ought not to do, lines beyond which humanity ought not to go. The startling and frightening advances of science in the last one hundred years have brought this question to the fore.

The discussion of the 'right and wrong', 'should and ought not', 'good and bad' of human action is properly the sphere of ethics, but it is all too frequently perceived to be the exclusive concern of philosophers and theologians. However, the extraordinary power of science to transform the world forces us to acknowledge that scientists cannot ignore the challenge that is involved in coming to grips with the ethical dimension of their work. Science is at the service of the human person in community, it is not and can never be conceived as an end in itself.

Particular questions to be resolved in this area would include the following: How do we know the good life or measure human progress: human flourishing, technological advances, material progress, human pleasure, contribution to individual happiness, promotion of the 'common good' and so on? Other questions might include: What does it mean to be a human person and do we own our bodies or how far have we the right to do what we want with our body? What are the limits to what we can do with the world and the universe? Has the human race any obligation for generations yet unborn? And if so, why? What do we mean by 'natural' and 'unnatural'? Have these concepts ethical implications?

Clearly, opposing views on the nature of the human being will suggest different responses to such questions. For example, the view that sees the human as only a material body will opt for physical and physiological good as the measure of human progress and welfare. On the other hand, the personalist or religious viewpoint will judge that a person's relationship with himself/herself, with others and with God is the core perspective within which all of human flourishing is to be assessed. A mature dialogue between science and religion provides the arena within which many of these opposing viewpoints can be named and it is only within such an environment that one can do justice to the complexity of the ethical issues confronting the contemporary world of science.

4.2   The Genetics Debate

Artificially created life
Just before midnight on July 25, 1978, Louise Joy Browne was born in Oldham District General Hospital in Greater

Manchester, England. Her birth was announced throughout the world, and the world's media have been present at many of her birthdays since. Indeed, the British House of Commons hosted a party on the occasion of her twentieth birthday in 1998. Why this extraordinary interest in the birth of a child? It was because Louise Brown was the world's first 'test tube baby'.

Two doctors, Patrick Steptoe and Robert Edwards, had spent almost a decade inventing and perfecting a technique for removing ova (eggs) from a woman's body, fertilising them on a culture dish (*in vitro* = on glass, in contrast to *in utero* = in a womb), and then replacing them in the mother's womb. Louise was the first such baby to be born. Since 1978, there have been 300,000 more such conceptions around the world. The technique, known as '*In Vitro* Fertilisation' or IVF for short, can help people with serious medical difficulties to conceive a baby.

The birth of Louise Brown brought to world attention both the great promise and the great threat of medical advances in the area of human reproduction. On one side, people marvelled at the joy the medical technique could afford otherwise childless couples. As Louise grew up and matured into a healthy adult, they had a living proof that science could sometimes get it right. On the other side, for the first time, doctors and scientists had 'played God'. They had produced a new human being by scientific process rather than by human intercourse. It had gone right, but it need not have. The phrase 'test tube baby' caught the public's hesitation nicely. Other reasons for hesitation, doubt, and misgiving were to emerge during the decades to follow. A boundary had been breached. Human life had been for the first time formed outside the human womb. What had been hitherto controlled by nature was now subject to human direction. The prospect of more innovations lay ahead.

The ethical responses to the new IVF technique reflected general approaches to questions of morality. Those who argued from a consequential standpoint saw the happy child and proud parents, an obviously good result, and so far as they could see, no bad results. Legalists relied on the absence of explicit legislation against IVF and regarded that as morally favourable. Situation ethicists saw the efforts of doctors and parents as clear evidence of love and therefore, morally laudable. Only those who regarded the action itself of moral significance, as opposed to its motives or its results or its circumstances, gave a negative judgement on IVF. The Catholic Church was one of these. In Catholic moral teaching the end can never be cited to justify the means, and the means in this situation were unnatural and unethical in the eyes of the Church. The operation on the woman to obtain ova was in order to overcome a medical difficulty, and that seemed to be justified, but the sperm was obtained outside intercourse and this represented an unjustifiable intrusion into the sacred space of human intimacy and God's special providence. In addition, the embryos created in excess of those needed for the actual uterine insertion were also of ethical concern. Catholics regard them as human beings. What was to happen to them, the moralists ask? Thus Catholic morality judged IVF to be immoral.

In the case of Louise Brown, the semen and ovum had been obtained from a man and woman who were the legal parents of the child, and the embryo had been replaced in the biological mother's womb to carry on the process of gestation. But this need not have been the situation, something that raises core issues concerning the nature of human parenthood, surrogacy and the rights of the child.

We will discuss this and other issues under the following headings: the status of the fertilised ovum, parenthood and surrogacy, reproduction outside the natural limits and human stewardship and co-creation.

Status of the fertilised ovum

When does a human individual begin? Moralists have wrestled with the dilemmas thrown up by the status of the fertilised ovum, whether inside or outside the womb. Ethical issues include the following; when does one become a bearer of human rights? (fertilisation, implantation, primitive streak, birth, etc.); what does it mean to be a person and when does personhood begin? The stance adopted here has implications for a range of issues in this area: discarding and/or freezing 'surplus' fertilised ova, the creation of fertilised ova for experimentation or research purposes. The Catholic (and Christian) position is that human life, and therefore, the human being as a person begins at fertilisation, the union of the semen and ovum. Modern biology would seem to lend support to an unbroken continuum from fertilisation to the mature adult. Some ethicists, however, argue for later times for the beginning of the human being. Four of these are implantation, the appearance of the 'primitive streak', viability and birth.

The technology of fertilisation and human reproduction introduces even more complications. The embryo can now exist outside the woman's body, preserved in a frozen state, and be exposed to medical procedures other than abortion. IVF, as practised, normally results in an over-production of embryos as doctors and scientists ensure against the failure to fertilise. Whether or not one considers IVF in itself to be moral, there is the fact that many fertilised embryos are now preserved in many laboratories and medical facilities outside the womb. What should be the fate of these embryos if, in the end, they are not going to be implanted in human mothers? What ethical protection should be accorded to these embryos, given that they have not been implanted, and therefore not involved in any particular woman's right to bodily integrity? Might not such an embryo possess a definite right to life, even in the view of someone who is in favour of the abortion choice for women? There are, after all, in this situation, no conflicting rights from a mother. For those who oppose abortion, of course, the embryo preserved in the laboratory is sacred and absolutely deserving of respect as a human being.

Another procedure involves the screening of fertilised embryos for abnormalities prior to implantation. Embryos identified as carrying disabilities are discarded as not suitable for implantation and reproduction. This appears to be a programme of eugenics: that is, formal screening and elimination of unsuitable candidates to produce improved offspring. Since the medical experiments in the Nazi prison camps during the Second World War, eugenics has aroused universal moral abhorrence. But the new reproductive technology has placed the real possibility of a new kind of eugenics in our hands – with associated moral questions.

Surrogacy and parenthood

Another situation arises where the embryo is implanted in a woman, not the biological mother, who then brings it to birth. This is called surrogacy. The surrogate mother can be acting for another woman or she can be acting for herself as the adoptive mother and the child she bears will be hers to rear.

The nature of parenthood is called into question here. What is the significance of biological parenthood (the source of the semen and ovum), as opposed to the surrogate mother (who bears the foetus to birth), and the adoptive parents (who nurture and rear the child to adulthood)? The dilemma of the natural versus the adoptive parents had already arisen, but now there is the added problem of the surrogate mother. For instance, could the surrogate mother at a later stage claim the child as her own? Or more seriously, change her mind during the pregnancy and arrange an abortion? Is the foetus hers or not? Some legal jurisdictions regard the surrogate mother's rights as prevailing over the biological parents. It goes without saying that religious people who consider the foetus a human being would not admit an abortion by anyone as moral, but what is their view of the relationship between the child and the surrogate mother? Judaism, to take one example, would seem to favour parentage, on the mother's side, being determined by the womb rather than the ovum.

Reproduction outside the natural limits

The most difficult problems attend the question of semen donation after death. Because of the new birth technologies, human beings are no longer limited by natural boundaries in reproduction. Women can bear children beyond menopause (the cessation of production of ova) because an ovum from the woman herself (stored from a previous procedure) or from another woman can be fertilised and inserted in her womb. This has already happened in Italy, and the news aroused a lively controversy. Was it fair of an elderly mother to have a child that she might find difficult to rear properly? The use of sperm preserved after the death of the father has been even more controversial. Should women be permitted to bear children with their deceased husband's sperm? What part should the husband's consent play in this? A particularly complicated situation known as the Del Rios Embryo Case occurred in Melbourne, Australia. The doctors had frozen embryos intended for *in vitro* fertilisation, but the parents were both killed in an airplane crash before they could be implanted and without leaving instructions for disposal of the embryos. What now could and should be done about them? The civil law could not decide it. Bernard Dickens expressed the legal dilemma: 'If the embryos are persons, they inherit their parents' estate; if they are property, the estate inherits them.' In the end (after a new law) the embryos were donated anonymously to a couple who wanted *in vitro* fertilisation. This illustrates the kind of ethical and legal problems that arise with fertilisation after death.

Human procreation and human reproduction

Christians approach such questions with a significantly sharp focus, because they have a strong sense of the participation of

God in the birth of any human being. They profess a belief that God creates each unique human soul. This places an emphasis on the sacredness of human intercourse and parenthood. Some Christian Churches celebrate marriage as a sacrament, a particular symbol of the divine. Hence, Christians tend to call the making of babies 'procreation', a sharing in the creative action of God. Obviously, this perspective stands in contrast to a medico-scientific standpoint on procreation, conveyed well by the scientific term 'reproduction'. In this context, it could be argued that IVF and its attendant technology of ovum storage and embryo preservation puts procreation in the control of science and technology, stripping it of the sense of the sacred and taking from human beings their sense of respect and dignity. In the light of these developments, it would seem timely that a fresh look be taken on the human respect and dignity that ought to be accorded to both the embryo and the foetus.

Genetically modified life

An article in the science journal *Nature* in April 1953 began with the sentence: 'We wish to suggest a structure for the salt of deoxyribose nucleic acid (DNA). This structure has novel features which are of considerable biological interest.' Those were the words with which James Watson and Francis Crick announced their momentous discovery of the double helix structure of DNA, which inaugurated a new era of molecular biology. They ended their nine-hundred-word presentation with what has been called the greatest understatement in modern science: 'It has not escaped our notice that the specific pairing we have postulated immediately suggests a possible copying mechanism for the genetic material.'

It is reported that Francis Crick had walked into the Eagle Pub in Cambridge on February 28th 1953 with the boast 'We have found the secret of life'. That sentence was probably as overstated as the previous one was understated; nevertheless, the discovery of the structure of DNA stands as one of the landmark discoveries of this or any age. Its promise drove biological research for the next fifty years, and is still driving it today. It opened up still unimaginable possibilities to take control of our lives. It has the potential, for good or ill, to change our life forever.

The research question for biology had been: how do living things reproduce themselves, passing on characteristics from one generation to the next? Crick and Watson's 'suggestion of a structure' that possessed a 'possible copying mechanism' was the key to further discoveries. The DNA molecule, as Crick and Watson explained it, comprises a 'double helix' structure with two strips of linked strands (like a twisted ladder). Every living species, animal or vegetable, has a genetic code in its DNA. Each gene has a specific function in determining the production of protein, and so guides the growth and development of the organism. The twenty-three 'rungs' of the human DNA 'ladder' form forty-six chromosomes containing approximately 30,000 genes. Each human being possesses a unique set of traits and qualities and so each individual human DNA is unique. And yet, the endless complications of the genetic code reduce to four base options only, an alphabet of four letters so to speak, repeated in endless variations of sequence: adenine (A), thymine (T), guanine (G), and cytosine (C). 'A' always goes with 'T' and 'G' always goes with 'C'. These four bases in their permutations produce the twenty amino acids that make up proteins, which in turn form the cell structure. The twisted ladder is also rather like a zipper. When it is 'unzipped', each side attracts its own matching base chemicals from the cell nucleus, and two identical 'zippers' result where there had been one. When the DNA has been copied in this manner, the cell divides, and this capacity for exact replication is, of course, the essential attribute of a living being.

A flood of new discoveries followed the Cambridge insights. The genes were variously described as the 'building blocks of life', the 'blueprints', and then lately, as the 'programme' or the 'wiring' to explain how growth and replication happened. Scientists continued to juggle the blocks, project the blueprints, interpret the programme and untangle the wiring.

In the 1970s scientists learned how to cut the DNA 'zipper' at designated spots, and insert new genetic material. This is called 'recombinant' DNA technology, and it meant that the genetic code could be changed, added to, and controlled in various ways. Scientists proceeded to experiment with animals and plants, and did indeed succeed in transferring genes from one species to another in both the animal and plant kingdoms. Human proteins were successfully produced in sheep milk, plants resistant to frost, drought or high saline soil were developed, and hopes are high that genetically altered plants could become a major source of vaccines, chemicals, or pharmaceutical products.

There have been two fears: an alarm about laboratory or environmental safety (whereby a new strain of bacteria, for instance, could damage people or organisms in the vicinity) and a horror of unpredictable long-term damage to genetic material. The first has been overcome with careful monitoring. The second has prevented scientists and doctors from intervening as yet in human sex cells or germ lines. Nevertheless, there is opposition and strong concern about any genetic modification of food (animal or plant). This opposition is based on 'naturalism' or a refusal to countenance any manipulation of nature. This is a religious or theological concern, if not always recognised as such, because it regards nature as of such ethical value that it ought not to be substantially altered. Scientists often see these objections as 'Luddite', meaning a conservative blindness to any progress and an irrational fear of innovation. There is merit in this point. Humankind has for millennia interfered with the natural reproduction of plants and animals, breeding and culling with great skill to arrive at the strains and varieties with which we are familiar today. The carrot and the cow, for example, are not found in nature in the form we have them now. But there is also an argument for caution with the genetic modification of nature. What makes genetic engineering different is the irreversible nature of intervention into the germ line (the sexual reproduction) of a species. This difference, however, would seem to demand prudent care, rather than outright condemnation.

Other calls for caution come from the blinding speed of genetic modification and the exponential knowledge explosion in biology. A final moral objection regards any exploitation of animals as unjust, as animals have their own dignity and worth, and may even be regarded as possessing rights. A belief in the superiority of humanity over all other species and therefore, the support of the human right to use animals for humanity's purpose is called 'anthropocentrism'.

Human gene manipulation is quite a different matter from animal or plant breeding, if for no other reason than mistakes cannot be so easily tolerated or disposed of. Another difference is that it involves intervention, manipulation, or one could say, intrusion into the sacred space of human intercourse and procreation, particularly when treatments involve the extraction of semen outside of intercourse, removing nuclei from embryonic cells, combining or splitting embryos, and selection or rejection of particular embryos. Nevertheless, the prospect of treating human genetic diseases or conditions is persuasive, if only because it would relieve so much pain and suffering.

From a religious standpoint, the faiths of Judaism, Christianity and Islam regard the human being as specially created by God, and therefore, deserving of much greater respect than animals or plants. The usual distinction of remediation *versus* improvement is applicable here. It is generally permitted morally to fix something that is defective, but not to augment or enhance something that is otherwise all right. So one would argue that genetic therapy, to cure a genetic disease, is justifiable, but action to enhance human qualities, even ones like intelligence or bodily structure, is not. James Watson's cynical question, however, shows how difficult a line this will prove to hold: 'If you knew how to do it, what woman would let her daughter be born ugly?'

The Human Genome Project

In 1988, humanity embarked on one of the most ambitious research programmes ever conceived: the Human Genome Project (HGP). It has been compared to splitting the atom or going to the moon. This was a plan to mobilise all the necessary resources to 'sequence and map' all the genes in human DNA, that is, to construct a huge data base – a kind of library – identifying and analysing all the genes in the human being, and making it universally available for medical and scientific research. A number of ethical issues come to mind, the first being that one's life is determined by one's genetic make-up and that therefore we cannot be held to be responsible for our actions.

This first issue concerned 'the gene myth' or 'geneticism'. This is the belief that 'It is all in the genes.' Just as the stars were once thought to control human destiny, some people today regard the genetic imperative as determining what human beings do. Although this denial of human freedom remains implausible, it will certainly prove to be the case that, with the advance of genetic research, certain genetic codes will be found to impel individuals in predetermined ways. This will have major impact on our legal and justice systems, and our moral thinking.

If, for example, a gene or set of genes associated with a particular illness or a criminal activity is successfully isolated, that information would be important both to the individual and society. A pertinent example is the chromosome connected to violence. If a child is identified as possessing this predisposition, society might want to intervene in his life intrusively, confine him, train him, and point his life in a particular way. This raises moral questions, because, presumably, the identification of the presence of the gene could pre-date any of his overt behaviour by a matter of years. Another example concerns the 'gay gene' as it has come to be called. There is, by all accounts, a possible genetic cause for male homosexuality, according to a team of researchers at the US National Cancer Institute. Questions arise as to what the individual will do, if he becomes aware about the homosexual gene that he possesses, or what society should do, were the information to be divulged. Consideration of the insurance industry, for example, will alert us to the prospect of companies weighing their risk exposure, and loading their premiums, or refusing coverage altogether according to the genetic profile of their clients.

These ethical concerns, naturally enough, go to the heart of information and knowledge. Is there knowledge that it is better for us not to know? That dilemma confronts all counsellors and many medical personnel when faced with a sick or dying person. The duty 'not to harm' may conflict with the duty to 'tell the truth', or at least, 'the whole truth'. These dilemmas are going to be particularly acute when health workers know genetic information, maybe about the health or future prospects of an infant, revealed during a pre- or post-natal screening. The limits of what should be made known to the parents and relatives, to the person, and to the civil and medical authorities have to be ascertained. Indeed, there is a prior question of how much *should* be uncovered during such a screening. There is a moral and economic argument that no more should be sought to be known, than can effectively and ethically be acted upon.

Cloning

The word 'Cloning' became a household term in February 1997 with the announcement of the birth of Dolly the sheep, the first successful animal clone, at the Roslin Institute in Edinburgh, Scotland by Ian Wilmut. The Roslin team achieved it by somatic cell nuclear transfer, that is, by transferring the nucleus of an adult body (somatic) cell into an ovum from which the nucleus has been removed, so that the embryo became a genetic copy of the adult donor. The breakthrough in this procedure was that the adult body (somatic) cell and its DNA had already been differentiated (specialised to be a particular part of the sheep's body) but the Scottish scientists had managed to change it to work as the nucleus of an undifferentiated embryonic cell. Accordingly, it was clear that in theory at least, any adult body cell could become the genetic material for a cloned organism. In fact, cloning of a higher mammal or human being can be accomplished in one of three ways: the 'Dolly method' (somatic cell nuclear transfer), embryo splitting (which occurs naturally with identical twins, triplets and so on, but can be induced artificially *in vitro*), and by the use of human embryo cells (undifferentiated cells). Only the Dolly method, of course, copies an adult organism.

All the methods involve manipulating embryonic cells outside the womb. Whatever about our ethical stance on animal experimentation, intervening in human embryonic development is a more serious ethical problem. As explained previously, ethicists differ on the moral status of the human embryo. For some, the embryo possesses the status of a human person. For others, the embryo is deserving of special moral respect. For still others, the embryo is simply a piece of human tissue, no more special than any part of the body. One's attitude towards research and experimentation and, indeed, any extra-uterine (outside-the-womb) procedures involving embryonic material from human beings depends on one's viewpoint on the moral status of the human embryo.

Reproductive and therapeutic cloning
There are two reasons doctors and scientists propose for cloning human embryos: reproductive cloning and therapeutic cloning. Reproductive cloning is directed towards producing offspring genetically identical to the cell donor. The purpose of

therapeutic cloning is to produce embryos for research or to grow products for medicinal purposes, such as human bodily organs for transplantation. The former points to a future in which people will be able to choose exactly what qualities they want for their children, gender, intelligence, appearance, and so on, in effect, 'designer babies'. Therapeutic cloning points to a time when bodily tissue could be produced at will for the purposes of the treatment of an illness. The moral issue can be put succinctly: is it ever ethically permissible to use and destroy an actual or potential human being for the good of another?

Discussion of therapeutic cloning often centres on a particular kind of embryonic cell called a 'stem cell'. Differentiated adult somatic cells, as we have seen, are ones that are already specialised for particular parts of the body. An embryo, on the other hand, contains undifferentiated cells – which have the ability to become any one of a range of different specialised cells – or stem cells. These are the ones, which scientists regard as more valuable for regenerating human tissue or growing into particular organs. This is the motivation for producing a cloned embryo for therapeutic purposes using the DNA of the adult. From the perspective of those who regard the embryo as having the status of a human being this procedure is unethical. The 18th century German Lutheran philosopher Immanuel Kant's dictum comes into play here: *Act so as to use humanity whether in your own person or in others, always as an end, and never merely as a means.*

There are, however, other possible sources for stem cells. They can be isolated from adult somatic cells without involving a new embryo, for instance from the bone marrow, though it is feared that these may be somewhat differentiated and not as capable to be turned in every direction as a true embryonic stem cell. A third source is the blood from a baby's umbilical cord just after birth. It could well happen soon that a baby's umbilical blood will be routinely frozen and stored for the particular person's future use in the case of necessity. Either of these last two sources would be ethically preferable because they do not involve the destruction or killing of an actual human embryo.

Prolonging or ending life?

Tony Bland set out on Saturday to go to a football match, a Cup Semi-Final between Nottingham Forest and Liverpool. The match was in Hillsborough in Sheffield and the date was April 15th 1989. At the start of the game, at five minutes after three o'clock, a crush of 5000 people at the Liverpool end of the ground in a narrow entry way resulted in the death of 95 fans. Tony Bland ended up in a bed in Airedale General Hospital in what was called a 'persistent vegetative state'. His chest was badly crushed, but he had been resuscitated on the pitch. His eyes opened and shut, he yawned and moved reflexively and randomly, and he reacted to loud noises. His bodily organs worked without any artificial assistance. But as far as anyone could ascertain, he could not perceive, think or feel. He certainly could not communicate with others. He had to be fed artificially with food and water through a tube in his nose. As this condition remained for many months, stretching into years, the doctors decided to withdraw nutrition and hydration, in other words, to stop feeding Tony and stop giving him water. They had recourse to the courts to permit them to do this. The case went through the High Court, the Court of Appeal, and the House of Lords. Finally in March 1993, the House of Lords agreed, the nasal tube was withdrawn and Tony Bland died nine days later. He was 22 years old.

The Tony Bland case illustrates graphically many of the questions raised by the medical treatment of dying patients. The general moral principle is that medical treatment should 'prolong life, not the process of dying.' There are two possible situations. The first one is this. With modern technology such as respirators, people can be kept alive for extended periods of time when, without the technology, they would certainly die. In this situation, it is clear that the machinery is prolonging the process of dying. The second situation arises when there is some hope that the person may pull out of the decline if kept on the machinery, and in the end, make some kind of recovery. In this case, the medical treatment plays a part in genuinely prolonging life. The doctor must judge the line between these two situations.

Another instructive case of this kind occurred in the United States. Karen Ann Quinlan went into a coma after taking alcohol and tranquillisers at a party on April 15th 1975. She was on a respirator to assist her breathing. She had no awareness of anything around her. Though she had reflexive movement, reacted to light and sound, grimaced and made some cries, she had no communication with anyone. Her doctors judged that she would never recover, but at best would remain in a persistent vegetative state in the life-sustaining machinery. Her family petitioned the courts of New Jersey to allow the machinery to be switched off, because the doctors had decided that they were only preventing Karen's death, while neither prolonging her life nor enhancing her chances of recovery. After a trial, which excited worldwide interest, the court allowed the switch-off. When the machinery was stopped, Karen lived on, in a coma, for almost ten more years before she died on June 11th 1985.

The differences between Tony Bland and Karen Ann Quinlan are clear. Karen needed the machinery to survive, and in the best judgement of the medical staff, was not ever going to recover. Tony did not need the machinery to survive (that is, he would not die without it) but he was never going to improve from the vegetative state he was in. Both, however, needed feeding through a tube to stay alive. The questions facing the doctors, the ethicists, the families, and ultimately, in both cases, the law courts were:

- Is feeding through a tube medical treatment? Or is it part of the normal duty of care extended to anyone?

- Is someone in a 'persistent (or permanent) vegetative condition' dead?

The answers to both are highly disputed. We will respond to the second question first. The usual signs of death are a stop to the heart beating and the lungs breathing, and the stop of brain stem activity. It is possible at times to resuscitate a patient whose heart and breathing have stopped, but if oxygen does not reach the brain through respiration and circulation (lung and heart action) through an extended period of time, there will be permanent brain damage, and eventually the brain waves will stop. This cannot be reversed. The case of both Tony Bland and Karen Ann Quinlan was that heart and lung action had stopped for a while, there had been serious brain damage, removing cognitive and affective responses, but brain activity had not completely stopped and they obviously kept on breathing and their hearts kept beating (Karen Quinlan needing machine assistance). It seems therefore that in both cases of persistent vegetative state, the patients were definitely not dead, but that one would die if the machinery were switched off. The moral upshot is that Karen eventually died naturally without the machinery as her doctors had predicted, but Tony had to be deliberately deprived of sustenance to end his life. It is this act of deliberately depriving him of sustenance that many regarded as ethically questionable.

This brings us to the second question. Is tube feeding a medical treatment parallel to the respirator in the Quinlan case? The UK courts ultimately answered that tube feeding is a medical treatment because it is 'artificial' and the person could not swallow safely unaided. Many medical ethicists and religious bodies, including the Catholic Church, however, hold that feeding and giving fluids is a normal duty of care, and does not constitute a medical treatment. The reasons are that it does not need a doctor to carry it on, and there are other situations when 'artificial means' are used for feeding, for example, baby bottles.

The obligation to prolong life
The significance of the discussion about 'medical treatment' lies in an analysis of the obligation to prolong one's life. The usual way of expressing this duty is to say that one should preserve and protect one's life using all 'ordinary' means. 'Extraordinary' means are optional. For instance, if one contracts a terminal cancer, and then hears that there is a rare and expensive and experimental cure on offer in a foreign country, there is no obligation to try it. It is too burdensome and risky, and certainly out of the ordinary. One may try it, but is not obliged to do so. This distinction between 'ordinary' and 'extraordinary' is all very well in theory, but with the rapidly changing capabilities of medical practice, it is difficult to determine which treatments are 'ordinary' and which 'extraordinary' at any particular time. An appendix operation for example was certainly extraordinary in 1900. It would be very ordinary and routine today.

If tube feeding were not medical treatment, but part of the normal duty of care for a patient, it should not be interrupted. To withdraw such care would be tantamount to starving the patient. If it were medical treatment, the question arises whether it is ordinary or extraordinary. A respirator is extraordinary, if necessary to keep a patient breathing for an extended period of time. Tube feeding, however, is now pretty ordinary and routine and not very expensive or burdensome. Hence the moral disquiet, and indeed, alarm at the decision of the Law Lords in the Tony Bland case.

Because of the difficulties attached to the 'extraordinary-ordinary' distinction, the Catholic Church in a Vatican document on Euthanasia (1980) has linked it with the concepts of disproportion and proportion. The document cites 'the type of treatment to be used, the degree of its complexity or risk, its cost and the possibilities of using it, and comparing these elements with the result that can be expected, taking into account the state of the sick person and his or her physical and moral resources.'

The ending of life and the right to self-determination
A pertinent factor in all of these discussions is the free choice of
the patient, and of the family or next of kin in the absence of
the patient's aware choice. One of the fundamental values in
Christian, and in contemporary, moral thinking is the freedom
of the individual. The Vatican Document on Euthanasia lays
emphasis on the importance of involving the patient and the
patient's family in the determination of what is to be done.
Whatever the medical or personal crisis, patients ought to be
directly involved in it as far as possible, take active responsibility
for their own life, and actively participate in decisions relating
to their welfare. It is particularly important to include the
patient and family in so-called 'quality of life' questions.

Doctors and medical personnel often argue that the
patient's prospective 'quality of life' does not warrant keeping
the patient alive. The moral problem attached to this argument
is that it is exclusively utilitarian – it judges the patient's life
according to criteria such as pleasure, capacity, breadth of
experience, and so on. What the patient may be able to do and
to experience becomes the measure of what the patient ought
to be. Furthermore, this measure accentuates those aspects of
life visible to others, judges unfavourably the interior and
spiritual life, and discounts entirely the value of suffering and
sacrifice. It also easily crosses over into the difficulties
experienced by the family and supporting community. Just
because it is burdensome and onerous for relatives or caregivers
to undertake the feeding and long-term care of an elderly
person is no argument for the termination of that person's life.
It is morally preferable that 'quality of life' issues be tackled
from the aspect of proportionality, that is, whether or not the
benefit or improvement in the patient's condition is worth the
cost of the proposed treatment. This, at least, avoids external
judgements and partisan evaluations of the value of human life
in general, and confines discussion to medical issues on which
doctors and medical personnel are qualified to pronounce.

Human autonomy and euthanasia

The question of self-determination and patient autonomy introduces a final medico-moral dilemma: euthanasia. Euthanasia comes from two Greek words meaning 'good death', and means advocating the right to suicide for terminally ill or extremely distressed patients if they want it. This includes the right to have doctors or others assist them in this project. The argument is based on the right to self-determination or autonomy for every human being. The nub is that many such patients are physically incapable of killing themselves effectively, either because they lack the mobility to acquire the necessary materials or the skill and strength to apply them adequately. Hence they need the assistance of some one else to accomplish their purpose. They usually identify their doctors, who are charged with their physical welfare, as the bearers of the duty corresponding to their right to self-destruction.

Traditionally, religions have condemned suicide or any kind of self-harming as immoral, and as a consequence, forbidden anyone to assist actively anyone attempting to harm oneself. Civil jurisdictions have regarded someone assisting another to commit suicide as guilty of homicide or murder. Hence, euthanasia advocates, and practitioners, like Dr Jack Kevorkian, have ended up in court, and judges and juries have found themselves adjudicating on these matters. Some have decided that euthanasia, though motivated by pity and mercy, is killing nonetheless. In a few jurisdictions, Oregon and the Netherlands to name two examples, euthanasia is permissible with certain safeguards.

Conclusion

Euthanasia is the result of an ethical framework relying on personal autonomy or individual choice as a foundation. Just as 'quality of life' decisions are utilitarian, euthanasia arguments are individualistic. We have noted, in this section of the book, a number of instances in which scientific techniques and medical procedures are moving off the page of traditional moral and philosophical/theological frameworks. The future will see even more examples of hitherto unimaginable possibilities. The past should convince us that just because something *can be* done is no evidence that it *should be* done. It is probably the case that public policy decisions in the future, especially those concerning advances in the area of health and human welfare, will need a more comprehensive and a more subtle awareness of both the medical science and the moral philosophy that should be their foundation. This is of course, a strong argument for the continuation of dialogue between science and religion.

Select bibliography

Cole-Turner, R. *The New Genesis: Theology and the Genetic Revolution*, Louisville, Kentucky: Westminster / John Knox Press, 1993

Cole-Turner, R. *Human Cloning: Religious Responses*, Louisville, Kentucky: Westminster / John Knox Press, 1997

Junker-Kenny, M. and Cahill, L. S. (eds) *The Ethics of Genetic Engineering, Concilium*, 2 (1998), London, SCM Press

Kushe, H. and Singer, P. (eds) *Bioethics: An Anthology*, Oxford: Blackwell, 1999

Peters, T. 'Genetics, Theology, and Ethics', and Clayton, P. 'Neuroscience, the Human Person, and God' in Peters, T., and Bennett, G. *Bridging Science and Religion*, London, SCM Press, 2002

Somerville, M. *The Ethical Canary: Science, Society and the Human Spirit*, Penguin Books, Ringwood, Victoria, Australia, 2000

Glossary

Anthropic Principle – the argument in cosmology that the initial structures of the universe were 'fine-tuned' such that it was inevitable that humankind would emerge.

Big Bang – the popular name for the Flaring Forth, the event fifteen billion years ago that marks the origin of our universe.

Conflation – the confusion or collapse of science into religion or religion into science so that their differences are blurred or lost.

Concordism – the effort to harmonise the findings of science with biblical texts, e.g. the six days of creation correspond to six geological epochs.

Consonance – the task of scientists-theologians today to relate theological teachings to the most contemporary scientific ideas.

Cosmology – the physics of the origin and structure of the material universe as a whole.

Creationism – the view that the Bible is a book of science; that it gives a better scientific account of the origins of the universe and life than evolutionary theory.

Deduction – the process of drawing conclusions from the most general principles rather than from the particulars of observation and experiment.

Deism – the belief that the world was created by God in the beginning, after which he withdrew and is not present in it anymore, as it runs according to its own laws.

Determinism – all events are subject to the laws of nature, following rigid causal pathways and allowing of no exceptions, and so theoretically predictable.

Dualism – Descartes' distinction between mind (unextended in space) and matter (extended in space), the object of science.

Empiricism – the view that all knowledge begins with sense experience, as opposed to rationalism.

Eschatology – religious teaching on the 'last things', referring to the final destiny of individuals and the world in general.

Fundamentalists – religious groups who believe in the literal interpretation and inerrancy of the Bible.

Genetics – the study of the chemical information that makes up the attributes of each living thing.

Genome – the chemical sequence of genetic information strung out along DNA.

Geocentric – the claim that the earth is at the centre of the universe, first held by the ancient Greeks and accepted by the Church in the Middle Ages.

Heliocentric – the claim that the sun is at the centre of the universe, first stated by Copernicus and defended by Galileo.

Hermeneutics – the study of the principles governing the interpretation of written texts, including the intentions of the author(s), and the social and historical context.

Holism – seeing the functioning of complex entities as a whole, rather than as the sum of their individual parts, as in reductionism.

Inerrancy – the fundamentalist belief that the Bible as the Word of God is without error in every detail, without which its authority would be undermined

Induction – the process by which knowledge is gained through the observation of particulars and moves to the construction of more general theory.

Indeterminacy – the openness of natural systems to a variety of outcomes at the quantum level.

Metaphysics – a part of philosophy that studies the most general principles about the nature of reality.

Model – an image or picture taken from everyday experience used to explain a more complex phenomenon in science.

Natural Selection – Darwin's theory that species evolve through the development of characteristics that enable individuals to survive and breed.

Pantheism – literally means 'God is everything', the belief that identifies God with the natural world; the denial of transcendence, that God is other than the world

Quantum Theory – a theory about unpredictability at the micro-level of particle physics and the influence of the observer.

Rationalism – the view that all truth has its origins in human reason (*ratio*) and not in the experience of the senses; reason can discover universal and necessary truths.

Relativity – Einstein's theories connecting space, time, mass and energy

Reductionism – the claim that the whole is nothing but the sum of the parts, that explaining how the smallest parts work is to explain the whole.

Scientism – the atheistic ideology which holds that science is the only reliable guide to truth; what science cannot measure does not exist.

Scientific Materialism – the atheistic ideology which holds that matter as described by science is the only fundamental reality.

Social Darwinism – the attempt to interpret social behaviour in terms of natural selection.

Theism – the belief in a personal God who is present in (immanent) but other than (transcendent) the world he has created.